"Martin Kutscher is a paediatric neurologist and understands the nature of ADHD as well as the perspectives and experiences of parents, teachers and children. He explains ADHD in a clear and engaging style that will ensure that his book will be read, appreciated and the practical strategies implemented at home and at school. I strongly recommend *Living Without Brakes* as the book of first choice for parents of a child with ADHD."

—*Tony Attwood, author of* The Complete Guide to Asperger's Syndrome *and* Asperger's Syndrome: A Guide for Parents and Professionals

"Dr. Kutscher has brilliantly accomplished exactly what he has set out to do. This book is wonderfully concise yet all-inclusive while remaining an easy read for parents and educators alike. The parenting and educational strategies are a great combination of proven methods that are realistic and practical to implement. Most of all, this book will help parents and anyone else who works with these children thoroughly understand how they think and why they function the way they do."

—*Heidi Bernhardt, National Director of the Centre for ADHD/ADD Advocacy Canada (CADDAC)*

"Even if parents, teachers, and therapists read no further than the table of contents, they will gain a hugely valuable set of guidelines for helping children with ADHD. Of course, they'd best continue reading, because Dr. Kutscher fleshes out each guideline in the realistic-but-optimistic style his readers have come to expect… I cannot imagine a more clear, concise, and empathetic guide. Reading this book is like sitting down for a leisurely chat with an extremely compassionate, informed, and down-to-earth physician."

—*Gina Pera, author of* Is It You, Me, or Adult ADD?

ADHD—Living without Brakes

by the same author

Kids in the Syndrome Mix of ADHD, LD, Asperger's, Tourette's, Bipolar, and More!
The One Stop Guide for Parents, Teachers, and Other Professionals
Martin L. Kutscher MD
With a contribution from Tony Attwood
With a contribution from Robert R Wolff MD
ISBN 978 1 84310 810 8

Children with Seizures
A Guide for Parents, Teachers, and Other Professionals
Martin L. Kutscher MD
Foreword by Gregory L. Holmes MD
ISBN 978 1 84310 823 8
JKP Essentials

of related interest

Dyslogic Syndrome
Why Millions of Kids are 'Hyper', Attention-Disordered, Learning Disabled, Depressed, Aggressive, Defiant, or Violent – and What We Can Do About It
Bernard Rimland
ISBN 978 1 84310 877 1

Understanding Motor Skills in Children with Dyspraxia, ADHD, Autism, and Other Learning Disabilities
A Guide to Improving Coordination
Lisa A. Kurtz
ISBN 978 1 84310 865 8
JKP Essentials

Parenting the ADD Child
Can't Do? Won't Do? Practical Strategies for Managing Behaviour Problems in Children with ADD and ADHD
David Pentecost
ISBN: 978 1 85302 811 3

Different Minds
Gifted Children with AD/HD, Asperger Syndrome, and Other Learning Deficits
Deirdre V. Lovecky
ISBN 978 1 85302 964 6

ADHD—Living without Brakes

Martin L. Kutscher MD

Illustrations by Douglas Puder MD

Jessica Kingsley Publishers
London and Philadelphia

First published in 2008
by Jessica Kingsley Publishers
116 Pentonville Road
London N1 9JB, UK
and
400 Market Street, Suite 400
Philadelphia, PA 19106, USA

www.jkp.com

Disclaimer
This information does not constitute medical advice, nor is it a substitute for discussion between patients and
their doctors. Medical information and recommendations are often subject to debate, and are likely to change
over time. This material is not intended to be all-inclusive. Full discussion of the approved indications,
usefulness, side effects, risks, monitoring, drug interactions, etc. of medications is beyond the scope of this
book. Not all of the medications discussed in this text have U.S. Food and Drug Administration approval for
use in children, or for some of the indications that they are commonly used for. Current detailed medication
information can be found from many sources, including your doctor, the manufacturer's package insert and
website, and the U.S. Food and Drug Administration website at www.FDA.gov.

Library of Congress Cataloging in Publication Data
Kutscher, Martin L.
ADHD - living without brakes / Martin L. Kutscher.
p. cm.
ISBN 978-1-84310-873-3 (hb : alk. paper) 1. Attention-deficit hyperactivity disorder--Popular works. I.
Title. II. Title: A.D.H.D.
RJ506.H9K883 2008
618.92'8589--dc22

2007031947

British Library Cataloguing in Publication Data
A CIP catalogue record for this book is available from the British Library

ISBN 978 1 84310 873 3

Printed and bound in the United States by
Thomson-Shore, Inc.

To the children who cope daily with problems they did not ask to have.

And to the people who believe in those children.

Contents

Success is When the Family Stays Together

It can be overwhelming. This thing we call "attention deficit hyperactivity disorder" (ADHD) is not just about cute kids with short attention spans. If that were the only problem in your life, you would not be reading this. ADHD is often about an overwhelmed kid who yells at his mother when she tries to help him. It is about mothers who fear that their relationship with their child is slipping away. It is about fathers who come home to find everyone at wit's end. It is about the threat to the most important things in life.

As I hear these stories over and over again in my practice in pediatric neurology, there are so many things I want to explain to families. I want to explain that the problems they are experiencing—the disorganization, the lack of planning, the living as if only the present moment exists, the overreactions, the screaming, the lying, the blaming others, etc.—are usually caused biologically as part of the condition we summarize with the letters ADHD. I want to explain behavioral approaches for home and school, and the role of medications.

I wanted a book that would concisely reinforce it all. I made many recommendations for the truly excellent books that exist. However, most times, the parent's response at the next visit was, "No, Dr. Kutscher, I didn't read those yet. If I had time in my life to read all of those 300-page books you recommended, I wouldn't have needed them in the first place!" Yet, the need existed. So, I scoured through the top books, condensed the best insights of brilliant thinkers, added some of my own, and wrote this text. The idea was to be brief, but not "dumbed down." Realistic, yet optimistic.

We begin with a discussion of the problems that we face: the full spectrum of ADHD and co-occurring symptoms. The chief difficulty is that people with ADHD cannot inhibit the present moment long enough to consider the future. It is not that Johnny doesn't care about the future; it is that the future and the past don't even seem to exist. Such is the nature of the disability (Barkley 2000). We'll also briefly discuss some of the mix of syndromes that frequently co-occur with ADHD, such as learning disabilities, anxiety, tics, Asperger's, and more. Let's not forget, also, that the ADHDer usually has a stressed out family to deal with as well.

The rest of the book deals with solutions. We start with a chapter on Rule #1: keep it positive. Although punishment can change behavior, only positive approaches can change behavior and improve attitude. Next is a chapter on Rule #2: keep it calm. No one can think clearly enough to logically solve problems when he is overwhelmed. Next we turn to, the school sphere of life, where we focus on Rule #3: keep it organized. Rule # 4: keep it going, is a brief reminder to keep doing Rules 1 to 3, because these biological issues can't be "cured" overnight. Then, we move on to the role of medications. We end with a summary recap chapter, which can also be read as a complete, freestanding text. The summary could be provided to teachers, spouses, and other family members. Finally, we conclude with checklists and further readings.

I am indebted to the original thinkers who have added so much to this field. I have cited their works when possible. I am further indebted to those people in my life who have added to my understanding of the full spectrum of ADHD. I hope that you find this book useful—and brief enough for you to actually read and use. The stakes are high: nothing less than our children's success, and our relationship with our children.

Good luck to your family. It will take time, but it can turn out great! Remember: The winner is the family that stays together (see Figure 1).

Figure 1: The winner is the family that stays together

Chapter 1

The ADHD Iceberg
More Problems Than We Expected

We've been missing the point

> Johnny is very active! He never stops moving. He gets distracted by
> any little noise, and has the attention span of a flea. Often, he acts
> before he thinks. His sister, Jill, is often in a fog. Sometimes, she's
> just so spaced that we want to call out, "Earth to Jill!"

That is how we typically consider children with attention deficit hyperactivity disorder (ADHD). OK, not so bad. But that is often only the tip of
the iceberg. Here is another likely description of the whole picture for a
child with ADHD:

> I can't take it any more! We scream all morning to get out of the
> house. Homework takes hours. If I don't help him with his work,
> he's so disorganized that he'll never do well. If I do help him, he
> screams at me. Since he never finishes anything, everyone thinks he
> doesn't care. No matter how much we beg or punish, he keeps
> doing the same stupid things over and over again. He never consid-
> ers the consequences of his actions, and doesn't seem to care if they
> hurt me. It's so easy for him to get overwhelmed. He is so inflexible,
> and then blows up over anything. It gets me so angry that I scream
> back, which makes everything even worse. Now that he's getting
> older, the lies and the cursing are getting worse, too. I know he has
> trouble paying attention, but why does he have all of these other
> problems as well?

It is not a coincidence that children with ADHD often manifest so much more than the classic triad of inattention, impulsivity, and hyperactivity. When we focus merely on these typically defined symptoms, we fail to deal with the whole vista of difficult problems experienced by patients and their families. This spectrum includes a wide range of "executive dysfunction" (such as poor self-control and foresight), additional co-occurring disorders of what we call the "syndrome mix" (such as anxiety, depression, or conduct disorders), and family stresses. These are summarized graphically in Figure 2.

Redefining ADHD to include "executive dysfunction"

ADHD needs to be redefined to include a wide range of "executive dysfunction." As Russell Barkley (2000) explains, this dysfunction stems from an inability to inhibit present behavior so that demands for the future can be met.

So, what are executive functions?

When you step on a snake, it bites. The snake has no "plan." No verbal discussion occurs within the snake's brain. No recall of whether striking back worked in the past. No thought as to where this action will lead in the future (such as making the next human even more likely to be cruel to snakes). Indeed, there is no inhibition: stepped on, bite back. Humans, fortunately, have the option to modulate their behavior.

No single part of the human brain is solely in charge of this self-control and planning. It does appear, however, that our frontal and pre-frontal lobes act largely as our "chief executive officer" (CEO). Orchestrating language and memory functions from other parts of the brain, these frontal centers consider where we came from, where we want to go, and how to flexibly control ourselves in order to actually execute the plan. These skills are called "executive functions." Specifically, executive functions identified by Barkley (2000), Brown (2005), and others include:

☐ *Inhibition* (putting brakes on your behavior) is the key executive function. Successful execution of a plan largely involves putting brakes on distracting activities. These brakes—courtesy of our

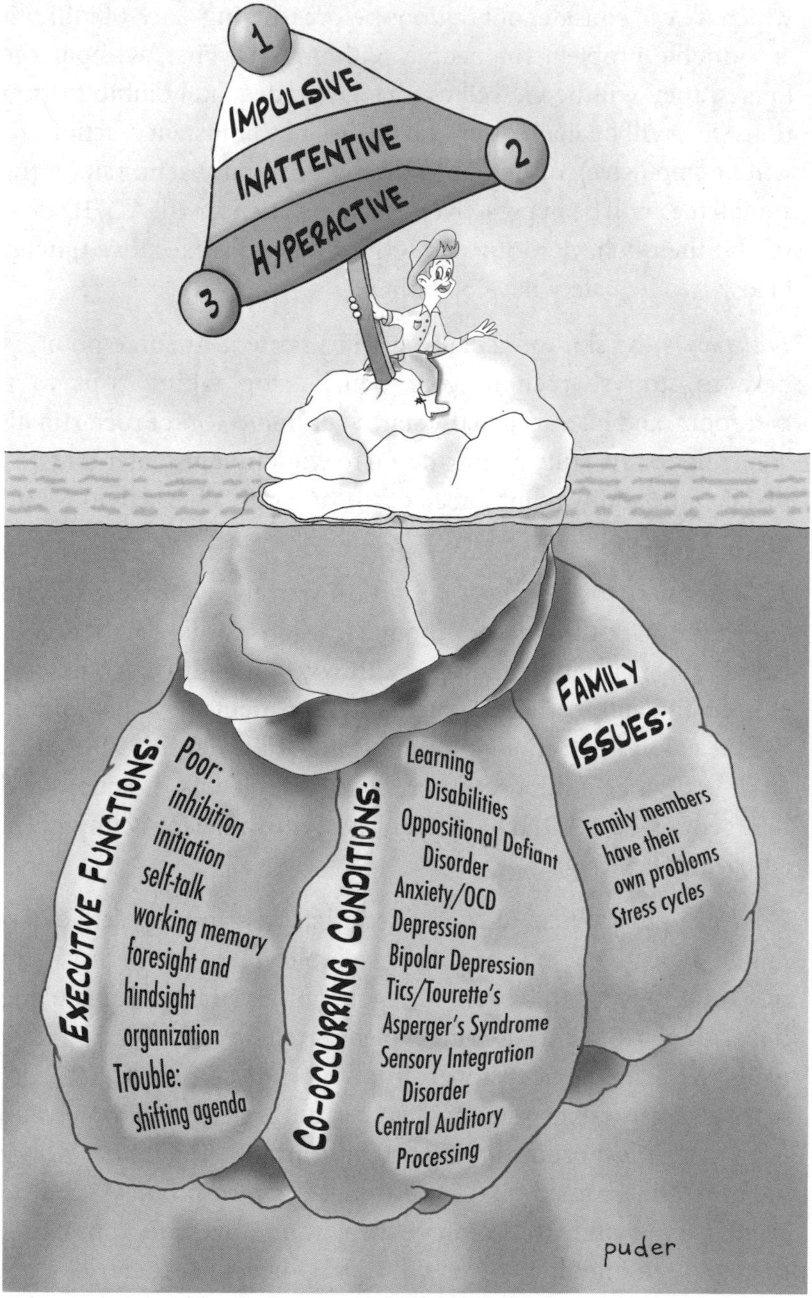

Figure 2: *Classically defined ADHD is just the tip of the iceberg. We also need to consider other executive function problems, co-occurring conditions, and family stresses*

pre-frontal inhibitory centers—allow us the luxury of time during which we can consider our options before reacting. Lack of inhibition is a double problem for people with ADHD. First, without these brakes, they will be viewed as unable to adequately inhibit distractions (i.e., will be inattentive), unable to inhibit instant reactions (i.e., will be impulsive), or unable to inhibit physically acting upon these stimuli (i.e., will be hyperactive). Second, patients with ADHD do not inhibit their behavior long enough for the other executive functions below to adequately develop either.

☐ *Initiation* is the skill of actually getting started. At some point, you have to stop sharpening your pencil, stop taking trips to the bathroom, and instead actually start your homework. Procrastination comes naturally. Truly getting down to work (not just intending to do it!) takes the ability to inhibit all of the other possible activities, and is tough for people with ADHD.

☐ *Self-talk* refers to the ability to talk to ourselves—a mechanism by which we work through our problems using words. Toddlers can be heard using self-talk out loud. Eventually, this ability becomes internalized and automatic. However, ADHD patients have not inhibited their reactions long enough for this skill to fully develop. Without the ability to either inhibit reactions or to use self-talk, it is no wonder that people with ADHD are impulsive (which means acting quickly and without thought).

☐ *Working memory* refers to those ideas that we can keep active in our minds at a given moment. For example, in order to learn from mistakes, we have to be able to juggle not just the present situation, but also keep in mind past times when certain strategies did or did not work. Working memory hopefully also includes keeping future goals in mind (such as remembering that we want to get into a good college, not just do the most intriguing activity currently available). Working memory allows us to take apart the pieces of a problem, and hold them in mind while we rearrange them into a novel solution. Without the ability to inhibit, people with ADHD never get to develop good function of their working memory. Planning and problem-solving skills will be hurt.

☐ *Foresight* (predicting and planning for the future) will be deficient when inadequate working memory teams up with a poor ability to inhibit the present distractions. People with ADHD cannot keep the future in mind. They are prisoners of the present; the future catches them off guard. In fact, surprisingly poor foresight is perhaps the greatest difficulty in their lives.

☐ *Hindsight* (remembering past experiences) is necessary if we are to gain wisdom from our past experiences in life. As we approach each current decision, it is helpful to recall which strategies in the past did and did not work. A lack of hindsight is one of the reasons that ADHD people tend not to learn from their mistakes.

☐ *Sense of time* is an executive function that is usually extremely poor in ADHD. The time estimates of ADHDers are notoriously poor—both too short and too long.

☐ *Organization* is a skill. Some people are good at it. ADHD people are not, almost by definition. As we shall see later, five out of the nine possible criteria for the inattentive category of ADHD are purely organizational—and you only need to meet six of the criteria to qualify for the diagnosis of ADHD.

☐ *Flexibility* is the skill to alter plans mid-stream as the circumstances change. The world is an unpredictable place, and plans rarely proceed just as we had imagined. Stuff happens along the way. We need flexibility to readjust our actions in mid-course.

☐ *Shifting from Agenda A to Agenda B*, especially at the behest of someone else, is a difficult task requiring good executive function. Pulling yourself out of one activity and switching to another—transitioning—is innately difficult, and requires effort and self-control. This inability to shift agenda (e.g., stop what you are doing and come to dinner) is a frequent cause of outbursts in ADHDers.

☐ *Separating emotion from fact* requires time to reflect. Neurologically speaking, each event in our lives has an objective reality, and an additional temporal lobe "emotional tag" which we attach to it. For example, we might return to our car and find a parking ticket on the windshield. Our emotional reaction might be absolute outrage over getting a ticket, but the objective fact is that the ticket was only for five dollars, anyway. Without the gift of time, we never get to separate our huge emotional feeling from what is really a tiny problem. We think that something really bad happened to us when it really didn't. This leads to poor ability to judge the significance of what is happening.

☐ *Adding emotion to fact* is an important part of "motivation." After all, it's hard to be motivated if you have no emotions attached to the activity at hand. So, working memory hopefully will recall not just the objective factual reality of past experiences and future hopes, but also recall the emotional tag that went along with that reality. For example, when recalling a past punishment, ADHDers may have trouble recalling the terrible feeling that accompanied it; and when recalling a previous great report card, they may have trouble re-experiencing the wonderful feeling that came with that. So, when ADHDers experience poor working memory, they may not recall the rousing emotions that should have come up with the facts—and may find themselves frustratingly detached and "unmotivated."

In short, then, the ability to modulate behavior comes largely from our frontal and pre-frontal lobes, which function primarily as inhibitory centers. Without the luxury of inhibitory brakes, not only will ADHDers act in a brakeless fashion, but they will not get to fully utilize any of their other frontal lobe executive functions, either.

What are the different kinds of problems in ADHD?

People with ADHD typically experience problems in three domains: (1) executive function; (2) co-occurring conditions; and (3) family stresses. Let's look at each domain in more detail.

1. Symptoms of executive dysfunction

In the previous section, we defined the components of executive dysfunction in scientific terms. Now, let's translate these problems into real life symptoms. As we shall see, redefining ADHD to include inadequate inhibition explains a wide spectrum of the everyday difficulties experienced by people with the syndrome. This expanded spectrum of symptoms can create an environment of havoc. For more details, the reader is referred to the important and inspired works by Barkley (2000, 2005), Greene (2005), and Silver (1999).

The author's Childhood Index of Executive Function (ChIEF©) scale in Appendix 2 will help the reader think about her own child in light of executive functions.

A. CLASSIC SYMPTOMS OF ADHD

ADHD is typically defined as a triad of inattention and/or impulsivity /hyperactivity. Box 1 is a somewhat simplified version of the official US DSM-IV criteria for ADHD as defined by the American Psychiatric Association (2000). These are the symptoms that receive the most attention from doctors, and all come from an inability to inhibit:

- *Distractible* ← inadequate inhibition of external stimuli.

- *Impulsive* ← inadequate inhibition of internal stimuli.

- *Hyperactive* ← physically checking out those stimuli.

B. OTHER SYMPTOMS OF EXECUTIVE DYSFUNCTION

If we do not address the following additional resulting executive function issues, we are only dealing with the tip of the iceberg. These are not just "incidental" symptoms. They are hard to live with—just ask the patient, his family, or his teachers.

It is *essential* to recognize that these difficult behaviors are typically built into an ADHDer's life. Otherwise, we will think that we have a child/student with ADHD who incidentally shows horrible self-control—not recognizing that these symptoms are all part of the same neurological package of ADHD/executive dysfunction.

☐ *Act like moths*—attracted to the brightest light. ADHDers are like moths: they are always smack up against the brightest light. Sometimes, the brightest light is a videogame. Sometimes it is the shiny pen or the fascinating paperclip on the desk. Rarely will the brightest

Box 1 Simplified DSM-IV criteria for ADHD

Modified and reprinted with permission from the *Diagnostic and Statistical Manual of Mental Disorders*, Fourth Edition, Text Revision. (Copyright 2000). American Psychiatric Association. The wording has been simplified and the symptoms of disorganization have been grouped together and placed in bold by the author to demonstrate how much disorganization is built into the definition of ADHD.

A. Either (1) or (2)

   (1) Six or more symptoms of inattention

      (a) fails to give close attention; makes careless mistakes

      (b) difficulty sustaining attention

      (c) does not seem to listen when spoken to directly

      (h) easily distracted by extraneous stimuli

      (e) difficulty organizing tasks

      (d) fails to follow through (not volitional or incapable)

      (f) avoids tasks requiring sustained organization

      (g) loses things needed for tasks

      (i) often forgetful in daily activities

   (2) Six or more symptoms of hyperactivity-impulsivity

     Hyperactivity

      (a) fidgets/squirms

      (b) leaves seat

      (c) runs or climbs excessively

      (d) difficulty playing in leisure activities quietly

      (e) "on the go" or "driven by a motor"

      (f) talks excessively

     Impulsivity

      (a) blurts out answers before questions completed

      (b) difficulty waiting turn

      (c) interrupts or intrudes

B. Some symptoms present before 7 y.o.

C. Symptoms in two or more settings

D. Interferes with functioning

E. Not exclusively part of another syndrome

Using these criteria, *DSM-IV* defines three subtypes of ADHD:

ADHD, Predominantly Inattentive Type.

ADHD, Predominantly Hyperactive-Impulsive Type.

ADHD, Combined Type.

Note, that by current terminology, the term "ADD" no longer exists. Even if there is no hyperactivity, the diagnosis will still be "ADHD" of the Predominantly Inattentive Type. Sorry. I didn't make the rules.

light be a book report that is due in two weeks. Unfortunately, sometimes the brightest light is a bug-zapper (see Figure 3).

☐ *Able to focus on videogames forever,* but not on homework. (Dad says, "Don't tell me he has a short attention span!! He can play Nintendo™ forever!") ADHD doesn't mean that you can't pay attention. It means that you can't pay attention to anything that isn't the most fascinating. Like moths, if you leave ADHDers in front of the most amazing attraction (which for moths are lightbulbs, and for boys are anything with a screen), they will stay there—until something else becomes more interesting. When it comes to doing homework, even a piece of lint might qualify as more intriguing.

☐ *Trouble actually executing a task.* (Johnny finds himself saying, "I'm going to do it…I'm going to do it…Holy cow, I didn't do it!") Most kids with ADHD intend to do their homework. Their executive dysfunction in the area of actually initiating tasks, though, prevents the execution of the job. They are probably as surprised as anyone when the teacher asks for the homework and they realize they don't have it ready.

☐ *Poor organization.* ("Johnny, I can't believe that we spent hours fighting over your homework, and then you didn't hand it in!") The quite common ADHD symptom of doing homework and not giving it to the teacher can only be explained by an organizational disability. If the kid actually had been "lazy," the time to be lazy would have been before doing the homework. Once it was done, no typically

Figure 3: Kids with ADHD are like moths, attracted to the brightest light. Rarely, will that be their homework

functionng brain would fail to seek credit for it—even if only to allow the kid to get away with not handing in tomorrow's homework. Disorganization is a cardinal symptom of ADHD. It often looks like lack of motivation.

☐ *Inconsistent work and behavior.* ("Johnny, if you could do it well yesterday, why is today so horrible?") With 100% of their energy, ADHDers may be able to control the task that most of us can do with 50% of our focus. But who can continually muster 100% effort? As the joke goes: ADHD children do something right once, and we hold it against them for the rest of their lives (Barkley 2000).

☐ *Trouble returning to task.* ("Johnny, you never complete anything. You get distracted and don't bother finishing. You just don't care.") People with ADHD often can get through the major aspects of a project in a burst of energy, but have trouble returning to the task to mop up the less-intriguing finishing details.

☐ *Poor sense of time.* ("Johnny, what have you been doing all afternoon? You can't spend one hour on just the first paragraph!")

☐ *Time moves too slowly.* ("Mommy, shopping takes forever!")

☐ *Lack of foresight!!!* ("Johnny, you'll never be prepared for midterms if you spend the rest of the vacation playing videogames instead of studying. Why do you keep shooting yourself in the foot?") Foresight—the ability to predict the results of our behaviors—is a major adaptive ability of humans. We can run imaginary simulations of possible future outcomes on our brain's computer. Lack of use of this ability can be the most devastating part of ADHD. It's not that Johnny doesn't care about the future; it is just that the future doesn't even exist in his working memory. His radar into the future is broken (see Figures 4 and 5). Mothers are usually endowed with great foresight (verging on obsession) regarding their child's future happiness. They are often crushed as they watch their offspring repeatedly head down counter-productive paths. On any given afternoon, Johnny is angry that his mother won't let him watch television. Simultaneously, his mother is already planning Johnny's future divorce and getting fired—because no one else in the future is going to put up with this behavior. Now, Mom could probably calm down a little bit—Johnny will probably still get into college even if he doesn't hand in tomorrow's French homework. However, her ability to predict Johnny's future needs probably is more accurate than her son's.

☐ *Poor hindsight/trouble learning from mistakes.* ("Johnny, don't you remember the problems you had the last twenty times that you left the book report until the last night?") Unable to inhibit the present, Johnny cannot stop to consider lessons from the past. Poor hindsight is one of the reasons why punishment rarely solves the problems for ADHDers—they can't keep past repercussions in mind as they face the present.

THIS IS WHAT JACK SEES:

puder

Figure 4: Foresight...

Figure 5: ...people with ADHD can't see the future coming up

☐ *Live at the "mercy of the moment."* ("All Johnny can do is react to whatever is happening to him right then and there.") ADHD behaviors make sense once we realize that they are based on reactions taking only the present moment into account. Johnny does care about the future. He does appreciate all of the nice things that you have done for him in the past. It is just that, right now, the future and the past don't even exist. Such is the nature of the disability. Sorry.

☐ *Living by the "Four-Second Rule."* If you want to understand and predict an ADHDer's actions, simply ask yourself, "What would I do if I felt like the world was going to end in four seconds?" Really, what would you do? It probably wouldn't be your homework. And (ethics, aside) if you were caught in a lie—and there was no future reputation to worry about because the world was ending in four seconds—it probably wouldn't be to tell the truth, either.

☐ *Poor ability to utilize "self-talk"* to work through a problem. ("Johnny, what were you thinking?! Did you ever think this through?")

☐ *Poor sense of self-awareness.* When asked what he was "thinking," Johnny will probably answer, "I don't know." He's probably right. He doesn't know. After all, he never got as far as actually thinking. So, impulsivity (defined as acting quickly and without thought) in ADHD comes from two reasons: the kids aren't good at stopping (therefore, they act quickly), nor or at self-talk (therefore, they act without thought).

☐ *Poor reading of social clues.* ("Johnny, can't you see that the other children think that's weird?") Johnny is too overwhelmed to note other people's reactions.

☐ *Trouble with transitions.* ("Johnny, why do you curse at me when I'm just calling you for dinner?") Trouble shifting agenda at someone else's time frame is a major cause of ADHD blowups.

☐ *Hyperfocused at times.* ("When Johnny is on the computer, I can't get him off. And once his father gets his mind on something, off he goes!") Finishing up the details will likely still be a problem.

☐ *Poor frustration tolerance.* ("Johnny, why can't you even let me help you get over this?")

☐ *Frequently overwhelmed and angry.* ("Mommy, just stop. I can't stand it. Just stop. Please!")

☐ *"Hyper-responsiveness."* ("Mommy, you know I hate sprinkles on my doughnuts! You never do anything for me! I hate you!") Barkley (2000) uses the term hyper-responsiveness to indicate that people with ADHD have excessive (uninhibited) emotions. Their responses, however, are appropriate to what they are actually feeling. So next time you see someone "overreacting," realize that they are actually "over-feeling," and must feel really awful at that moment.

☐ *Push away those whose help they need the most.* ("Mommy, stop checking my assignment pad. Get out!") Simply overwhelmed.

☐ *Inflexible/explosive reactions.* ("Johnny, you're stuck on this. No, I can't just leave you alone. Johnny, now you're incoherent. Johnny, just stay away. I can't stand it when you break things!"). See Chapter 3 on staying calm.

☐ *Feels calm only when in motion.* ("He always seems happiest when he is busy. Is that why he stays at work so late?")

☐ *Thrill seeking behavior.* ("He feels most 'on top of his game' during an emergency. He seems to crave stimulation at any cost.")

☐ *Trouble paying attention to others.* ("My husband never listens when I talk to him. He just cannot tolerate sitting around with me and the kids. He doesn't 'pay attention' to his family any more than he 'paid attention' in school.") As the ADHDer gets older, people in his or her life will increasingly expect more time and empathy to be directed their way. Yet, the ADHD behaviors above may interfere with the demonstration of these traits, despite the passions of someone with ADHD.

☐ *Trouble with mutual exchange of favors with friends.* Friendships can be hard to make without establishing a reliable "bank account" of kept promises and returned favors.

☐ *Sense of failure to achieve goals.* ("Somehow, I never accomplished the things that I could have done.") This deep disappointment is commonly what brings adults with ADHD to seek help—along with recognizing their own symptoms when their child is brought to an evaluation.

☐ *Lying, cursing, stealing, and blaming others* become frequent components of ADHD, especially as the child gets older. According to some particularly depressing data by Barkley *et al.* (1990), here is how ADHD children compare to typical children:

- ○ 72% of ADHD children argue with adults (vs. 21% of typical children)

- ○ 66% of ADHD children blame others for their own mistakes (vs.17% of typical children)

- ○ 71% of ADHD children act touchy or easily annoyed (vs. 20% of typical children)

- ○ 40% of ADHD children swear (vs. 6% of typical children)

- ○ 49% of ADHD children lie (vs. 5% of typical children).

In short, the symptoms of ADHD become less "cute" as the children switch from elementary to secondary schools. The "good" news comes from understanding that these problems are commonly part of the syndrome we call ADHD. They are nobody's fault—not yours, and not your child's. This understanding points the way towards coping with these issues.

The neurological basis of ADHD: frontal lobes asleep on the job

If "official" US *DSM-IV* criteria are applied, ADHD occurs in roughly 6% of school age children no matter where in the world we look (Barkley 2000). Even though only about 6% (i.e., 1 out of 16) of children have the condition, it seems even more prevalent. That's because its presence of 1 out of 16 people means that one out of four families are affected by the condition (assuming roughly four people per family). Yes, if four mothers get together, then one of their households will be affected by ADHD. That's a lot of families.

True ADHD is a real biological condition. The current understanding can be summarized as follows:

- The frontal and pre-frontal lobes (conveniently enough, located in the front part of our brain behind the forehead) are the home of our executive and inhibitory functions.

- The neurotransmitters dopamine and norepinephrine play a major role in the inhibitory functions of these frontal and pre-frontal lobes.

- In ADHD, there is insufficient action by these neurotransmitters.

- People with ADHD show poor executive and inhibitory behaviors.

Simply put, in ADHD, the frontal lobe brakes and other executive functions are asleep on the job. You already know what happens when the frontal lobes are sleepy. Just think about how typical kids act when they are over-tired and their frontal lobes are not fully awake: at midnight, all six-year-olds are cranky and can't concentrate. Consider that tired secretaries who are in need of a coffee break stop working efficiently and get chatty. Further, look at what happens when people drink alcohol. Alcohol is actually a central nervous system depressant (the opposite of stimulants), and puts the frontal lobes to sleep. That results in the poor self-control, poor foresight, and over-talkative behaviors of people who consume alcohol. As we will see in the chapter on medications, stimulant medications work by increasing dopamine and norepinephrine levels, thus waking up the frontal lobe brakes.

ADHD and its treatment are the subjects of thousands of scientific studies. Adoption and other genetic studies, epidemiological studies, MRI studies, EEG studies, and PET scans all combine to give frankly incontrovertible evidence for the existence of this medical condition and the effectiveness of current treatments. Smith, Barkley, and Shapiro (2006) have discussed some of the peer-reviewed research findings in ADHD:

- SPECT (single-photon emission computed tomography) shows decreased blood flow to the pre-frontal regions (especially on the right).

- PET (positron emission tomography) scans show diminished glucose metabolism in adult frontal lobes.

- MRI (magnetic resonance imaging) scans show smaller anterior right frontal regions, along with smaller size of the cerebellar vermis and some of the basal ganglia to which they connect.

- fMRI (functional MRI) scans show abnormality in the same regions when ADHD children attend or inhibit.

- EEGs (electroencephalograms) show frontal lobe slowing and excessive beta activity (indicative of under-arousal of the frontal lobes).

- Twin studies show that genetic factors control up to 75 to 97% of a person's risk for ADHD.

- Psychological tests show poor working memory and other executive functions in ADHD patients.

- Biological factors in the environment associated with ADHD include lead exposure, prematurity at birth, low birth weight, and prenatal exposure to alcohol and tobacco.

In 1998, the American Medical Association concluded that ADHD has been one of the best-researched medical conditions, and that evidence for its validity are much more compelling than the evidence for most mental conditions and even many medical disorders (Goldman *et al.* 1998). Further, Smith *et al.* (2006, pp.73, 76) conclude that based on research: "purely social causes of ADHD can be largely ruled out as likely contributors to most forms of ADHD... Studies consistently find little if any effect for shared (rearing) environment on the traits of ADHD; this refutes an effort to attribute ADHD to poor parenting, family diet, household television exposure, or other popularly held causes for the disorder." In general, the only "blame" for these behaviors that you can pin on the parents is the contribution of their genes—but they didn't have much choice in that.

Medical conditions that can cause ADHD symptoms

There are a number of medical conditions that can mimic or cause ADHD symptoms. The first step in evaluating any of these conditions is a careful history and physical exam. These conditions include:

- thyroid disease

- iron deficiency or other types of anemia

- lead poisoning

- poor sleep—sleep apnea is suggested particularly by *loud* snoring, restless or apneic sleeping, or morning fatigue

- substance abuse

- seizures—absence seizures (previously called "petit mal") can present with periods of inattention and staring off blankly. They can often be distinguished from ADHD according to Table 1. Even an EEG, though, can fail to distinguish between these two conditions, especially if the EEG does not happen to capture a suspected spell. Rarely, subclinical seizures can occur during sleep at night and cause confusion and language problems during the day.

Besides these medical conditions, a host of neuro-psychiatric conditions can co-occur, worsen, or mimic ADHD. Let's turn to them now.

2. The "syndrome mix" of co-occurring disorders associated with ADHD

In addition to the executive dysfunctions above, there are myriad co-occurring disorders that frequently accompany the diagnosis of ADHD in the patient and/or her family. These disorders may often be misdiagnosed as ADHD, or they may coexist with true ADHD, or they may be worsening each other. In addition, many people are "subsyndromal," and have just parts of the following diagnoses. John Ratey (1998) refers to these as "shadow syndromes." Since 70% of children with ADHD children ages 7 to 9 meet criteria for another *DSM-IV* diagnosis (MTA Cooperative Group 1999), the presence of these disorders must be investigated whenever the diagnosis of ADHD is

Table 1 Distinguishing ADHD from seizures (Kutscher 2006)

Staring off in ADHD	Staring off in seizures
Occurs only during "down time," such as while watching television or bored.	Occurs any time, including in the middle of an activity, such as while talking or eating.
The spell stops when the child is called loudly or touched.	Touching or loudly calling to the child does *not* end the spell.
There are no associated symptoms.	There may be associated symptoms such as eye fluttering, lip smacking, or body twitching.

being considered. A screening checklist for such problems is found in Appendix 2. Sources of additional information on these conditions can be found in Appendix 3. Individual medications that might be used as part of the treatment of these conditions are discussed in Chapter 6.

A. LEARNING DISABILITIES (LD)

Brown (2005) concludes that 70% of children with ADHD have a learning disability. A review of the diagnostic criteria for ADHD (see Box 1, p.22) shows that a disability in the skill of organization is virtually built into the definition of ADHD. Particularly common disabilities are problems following directions, sequencing, written expression, and poor handwriting (dysgraphia). Learning disabilities should be suspected whenever a student does not "live up to his or her potential." They are identified by history, exam and psycho-educational testing. As well explained by Larry Silver (1999), learning disabilities can either exacerbate or mimic ADHD. After all, how long can someone focus on something that she does not understand?

B. DISRUPTIVE BEHAVIORAL DISORDERS

More than 50% of ADHD children meet criteria for a disruptive behavioral disorder (MTA Cooperative Group 1999). Even in the absence of a full diagnosis, the lives of many (if not most) children with ADHD are

This information does not constitute medical advice. Medication use in children is frequently done "off-label," and information is often quite limited. Not all of the medications discussed in this text have U.S. Food and Drug Administration approval for children, or for some of the indications that they are commonly used for. Recommendations need to be taken as subject to change and debate. See Chapter 6 on medications. This information is not intended to be all-inclusive. Full discussion of the usefulness, indications, side effects, risks, monitoring, drug interactions, etc. of these medications is beyond this book. Check with your doctor, the package insert, and www.FDA.gov for new and complete information. The reader is also referred to *ADHD with Comorbid Disorders* by Pliszka, Carlson and Swanson (1999), which forms much of the basis for the following medication assessments. Medical treatment of the associated disorders is perhaps best done in consultation with a neurologist or psychiatrist.

afflicted by lying, cursing, taking things that do not belong to them, blaming others, and being easily angered. This frequency is not surprising given the executive dysfunction hypothesis of ADHD. Full definitions of the disruptive behavioral disorders can be found in the Diagnostic and Statistical Manual-IV (American Psychiatric Association 2000). Medications such as Depakote™ (valproic acid), Catapres™ (clonidine), Tenex™ (guanfacine) and neuroleptics such as Risperdal™ (risperidone) can sometimes help with impulsivity and aggression.

The three conditions that comprise the disruptive behavioral disorders are:

1. Oppositional defiant disorder (ODD). Whereas ADHD children cannot comply because of inattention or impulsivity, ODD children are unwilling to conform (even with an intriguing task). They may be deliberately annoying, negative, belligerent, angry, or spiteful. Although many children with ADHD and mood disorders meet diagnostic criteria for ODD, I personally rarely diagnose the latter condition, instead finding most of the negative behaviors as inadvertently stemming from an overwhelmed nervous system. In other words, I see oppositional behaviors as usually secondary to

some other problem that has yet to be successfully addressed (see Table 2: ADHD vs ODD).

2. Conduct disorder (CD). Children with CD are more frequently overtly hostile and law breaking, with a lack of remorse that is not seen in ADHD alone. These people violate the rights of others, such as with physical cruelty to others or animals, stealing, etc.

3. Antisocial personality disorder. People with antisocial personality disorder have a pervasive pattern of severe violation of the rights of others, typically severe enough to merit arrest.

Table 2 ADHD vs. oppositional defiant disorder

ADHD	Oppositional defiant disorder
Poor compliance comes from being overwhelmed.	Poor compliance comes from unwillingness to conform.
Annoys others when overwhelmed.	Annoys others deliberately.
Remorseful for problem behaviors.	Gets a "kick" or a thrill out of watching others squirm.
Not spiteful.	Spiteful.

C. ANXIETY DISORDER

Anxiety disorder occurs in 34% of children with ADHD (MTA Cooperative Group 1999), but half of these children never tell their parents (Bernstein and Layne 2004)! Patients are beset most days by painful worries not due to any imminent stressor. They usually find multiple things to worry about, and dislike the fact that they are worrying so much. Children may appear edgy, stressed out, tense, or sleepless. There may be panic attacks. Treatments include the following:

- Change of environment, exercise, and meditation.

- Cognitive behavioral therapy (CBT) seems to be highly effective.

- Selective serotonin uptake inhibitors (SSRIs) such as Prozac (fluoxetine) Luvox (fluvoxamine), Paxil (paroxetine), Zoloft (sertraline) Celexa (citalopram), or Lexapro (the active half of Celexa) are quite effective.

- Buspar (buspirone)—helps anxiety but not panic attacks.

- Klonopin (clonazepam)—may help anxiety.

- Tricyclics—help some with anxiety and are great for panic attacks.

- Stimulants may directly worsen anxiety, but may help indirectly if the anxiety was created by issues related to inattention.

D. OBSESSIVE COMPULSIVE DISORDER (OCD)

Recurrent and intrusive obsessive thoughts, and compulsive actions (which are done in an effort to neutralize those thoughts), may occur in up to one-third of ADHD patients (Geller *et al.* 1996). If ADHD is living in the present, then anxiety/OCD is living in the future. Although difficult to live with, the future goal directed behavior of anxiety/OCD might help compensate for the organizational problems of ADHD. Cognitive behavioral therapy (CBT) seems to be very effective, and should probably be tried first, if available. Selective serotonin re-uptake inhibitors (SSRIs) are the current mainstay of medical treatment.

E. MAJOR DEPRESSION

Estimates for the co-occurrence of ADHD and depression are 15 to 75% of ADHD children and 47% of ADHD adults (Brown 2005). Although pure ADHD patients get depressed briefly, they flow with the environment (changing within minutes). In contrast, depressed children stay depressed for long periods. The symptoms include loss of joy, sadness, pervasive irritability (not just in response to specific frustrations), withdrawal, self-critical outlook, and vegetative symptoms (such as changes in appetite or sleep). Insomnia is a prominent marker for both depression and anxiety. Treatment may include:

- counseling and adjusting the person's environment

- selective serotonin uptake inhibitors (SSRIs)

- Wellbutrin (bupropion)—modestly helps both depression and ADHD, with limited data in children

- tricyclics (such as Tofranil and Pamelor) do not appear to work in children for depression in controlled clinical trials.

F. BIPOLAR DEPRESSION

Bipolar depression occurs in up to 16% of ADHD children (Pliszka *et al.* 1999). Classic bipolar patients may show depression cycling with manic (abnormally elevated, expansive, grandiose, and pressured) moods. Children may cycle within hours. Other hallmarks include severe separation anxiety and often precociousness as children; extreme irritability; extreme rages that last for hours; very goal directed behavior; and little sleep requirement. They may demonstrate hypersexuality; gory dreams; extreme fear of death; extreme sensitivity to stimuli; oppositional or obsessive traits; heat intolerance; craving for sweets; bedwetting; hallucinations; possible suicidal tendencies; or substance abuse. Often symptoms are shown only at home (see *The Bipolar Child* by Demitri and Janice Papolos, 2006).

The symptoms of ADHD can usually be found at some point in the life of a person with bipolar disorder. Thus, we need to always consider bipolar when a diagnosis of "ADHD" is being made, but especially if it is accompanied by the above symptoms or the following:

- Family history of bipolar disorder, substance abuse, or suicide.

- Prolonged temper tantrums and mood swings. Sometimes the angry, violent, destructive, sadistic, and disorganized outbursts last for hours (vs. less than 30 minutes in ADHD).

- Bipolar rages are typically from parental limit setting; in ADHD rages are from overstimulation.

- Oppositional/defiant behaviors.

- Explosive and "intentionally" aggressive or risk seeking behavior.

- Substance abuse.

- Separation anxiety, bad dreams, disturbed sleep; or fascination with gore.

- Morning irritability or immobility that lasts hours (vs. minutes in ADHD).

- Symptoms worsen with stimulants or antidepressants (see Table 3).

Medical treatments for bipolar depression include mood stabilizers such as lithium and valproate (Depakote/Depakene). Carbamazepine (Tegreto) clearly helps bipolar and aggressive symptoms at least in adults, but there is limited information in children. Neuroleptics such as risperidone (Risperdal) help with psychotic symptoms (such as hallucinations) and aggression. Stimulants and antidepressants may trigger mania, and need to be used with great caution if there is suspicion of bipolar disorder.

G. TICS AND TOURETTE'S (MOTOR AND VOCAL TICS)

Seven percent of ADHD children have tics; but, conversely, 60% of Tourette's patients have ADHD (Waslick and Greenhill 2004). Briefly defined, Tourette's is marked by year-long periods of at least one vocal tic (such as throat clearing or sniffling), and at least two motor tics (such as eye blinking or neck stretching). The first line of treatment is reassurance and not drawing attention to the tics. Medical treatments should be considered if the tics become socially disabling. Medications for tics include clonidine (Catapres) and guanfacine (Tenex), which help impulsivity and tics. Risperidone (Risperdal) and other neuroleptics are quite helpful. Note that stimulants may exacerbate tics (or sometimes secondarily improve them). Streptococcal and other infections may exacerbate tics or anxiety/OCD symptoms as part of an immune response called PANDAS (Pediatric Autoimmune Neuropsychiatric Disorders Associated with Strep).

H. ASPERGER'S SYNDROME

Tony Attwood (2007) concludes that 75% of people with Asperger's syndrome have ADHD. Symptoms of autistic spectrum disorders include

Table 3 ADHD vs bipolar disorder. A summary of Dr. Charles Popper's information as presented in Papolos and Papolos (2005).

ADHD	Bipolar
Tantrums occur when child is overwhelmed.	Tantrums occur when child is told, "No!"
Tantrums last less than 30 minutes.	Tantrums may last hours.
Tantrums are fairly mild.	Tantrums are vicious, cruel, mean, "go for the jugular," or disorganized.
Usually in a good mood until overwhelmed and then becomes easily irritated for brief periods.	Mood swings: walks around in a prolonged irritable state with a "chip on his shoulder;" or in a manic, pressured, excitable state.
Sleep problems usually limited to sleep onset insomnia. Wake up before dreams get gory.	Sleep problems include poor maintenance and limited need for sleep. Dreams may include actual gore.
Morning irritability is brief.	Morning irritability, sluggishness, and virtual immobility may last hours.
Risky behavior stems from lack of foresight.	Risky behavior stems from intentionally seeking a thrill.
Substance abuse in child.	Strong history of substance abuse in child or family.
Family history of ADHD.	Family history of bipolar ("manic-depression") or suicide.
No psychosis or hallucinations.	May include psychosis or hallucinations.
Stimulant medications help.	Stimulant medications may provoke mania.
Antidepressant medications may help associated depression or anxiety.	Antidepressant medications may provoke mania.
Hypersexuality, heat intolerance, cravings for sweets, separation anxiety, and fear of death are unusual.	Hypersexuality, heat intolerance, cravings for sweets, separation anxiety, and fear of death are common.

impaired ability to utilize social cues such as body language, irony, or other "subtext" of communication; restricted urge to socialize; poor eye contact; limited range of encyclopedic interests; perseverative, odd behaviors; didactic, monotone voice; "concrete" thinking; oversensitivity to certain stimuli; and unusual movements. See the leading works of Attwood (2007) and Bashe and Kirby (2001).

Distinguishing ADHD from Asperger's

ADHD and Asperger's share a number of common features. In both, there is trouble with self-talk, self-awareness, the reading of social cues, and the demonstration of empathy. Both groups generalize rules poorly, and do better with predictability and routine. Differences between ADHD and Asperger's are shown in Table 4.

Table 4 ADHD vs. Asperger's syndrome

ADHD	Asperger's syndrome
Have normal empathy, but trouble controlling their behavior long enough to show it.	Primary problem is with empathy.
Inattention is a primary problem.	Inattention sets in when the person doesn't comprehend what he is expected to do.
Tyrannized by disorganization and by not following rules.	Tyrannized by organization and by following rules.
Flies from one area to another.	Perseverative, narrow range of interests.
Oppositional while going to the brightest light.	Oppositional to avoid anxiety.

I. SENSORY INTEGRATION (SI) DYSFUNCTION

SI dysfunction (also recently called "sensory processing disorder," SPD) is the inability to process information received through the senses at the right "volume" level. The child may be either over-sensitive or under-sensitive to stimuli. Or, the child may not be able to process and execute a coordinated response to the sensory information. SI may mimic or coexist with ADHD. SI is typically evaluated and treated by an occupational therapist (see Kranowitz's book, 1998). Some types of SI include:

- hypersensitive to touch: sensitive to clothes, tags, or getting dirty; withdraws to light kiss

- hyposensitive to touch: seeks to wallow in mud or rub against things; unaware of pain

- hypersensitive to movement: avoids running, climbing, or swinging

- hyposensitive to movement: seeks crashing into things, rocking, twirling, or unusual positions

- may also respond abnormally to sights, sounds, smells, tastes or textures

- may be clumsy, have trouble coordinating (bilateral) movements, or have poor fine motor skills.

Table 5 ADHD vs. CAPD (from Kutscher 2005)

ADHD	CAPD
Difficulty attending to all non-intriguing tasks.	Difficulty attending to listening related tasks.
Background noise makes it harder to attend to the information.	Background noise scrambles the information.
Students typically can comprehend, once you get their attention.	Students may have trouble with comprehension of oral tasks, even once you get their attention.
Have executive function difficulties, such as organizational problems.	Executive functions are relatively intact, as long as the child understands the task at hand.
May be physically hyperactive, overreactive, or impulsive.	Unless acting out from academic frustration, students are not usually disruptive.
Typically do not have memory problems.	May have auditory memory problems.

J. CENTRAL AUDITORY PROCESSING DISORDERS (CAPD)

Central auditory processing refers to the steps taken by the brain to convert sounds into meaning. Symptoms of a central auditory processing disorder (CAPD) include trouble with comprehension of spoken information such as: following a sequence of directions, following long conversations, tolerating noise, and demonstrating worsened comprehension when faced with competing sounds.

CAPD frequently co-occurs with ADHD. To further confuse matters, CAPD shares some symptoms with ADHD: trouble concentrating on the main subject, trouble filtering out the background; and trouble following a sequence of directions. Distinguishing features are shown in Table 5. Detailed testing is done through specialized audiology evaluations.

3. Familial issues

These can be of two categories:

A. FAMILY MEMBERS WITH THEIR OWN NEURO-PSYCHIATRIC PROBLEMS

Family members may have their own ADHD, OCD, depression, anxiety, or other condition. In fact, a child with ADHD has a 40% chance that one of his parents has ADHD (Kutscher et al. 2005). Such difficulties affect the family's ability to cope with the ADHD child, and may need to be addressed independently.

B. STRESS—CREATED BY THE CHILD—CYCLING BACK TO FURTHER CHALLENGE THAT CHILD

Children or adults with ADHD can create chaos throughout the entire family, stressing everyone in the process. The morning routine and homework are frequent (and lengthy!) sources of dissension. Other siblings are often resentful of the time and special treatment given to the ADHD child. Mothers, who frequently consider their child's homework to be their own, find it stressful that "their" homework never seems to get completed. Fathers come home to discover a family in distress, and that they are expected to deal not only with a child who is out of control, but also with the mother who is understandably now losing it, too. Parents may argue over the "best strategy," a difficult problem since few strategies are even close to perfect. The unpleasantness of life around someone with ADHD leads to a pattern of avoidance that only furthers the cycle of anger. In turn, all of this family turmoil creates a new source of pressures and problems for the already stressed ADHD patient to deal with. The last thing an ADHD kid needs is a stressed out mom—even if the child is the source of that stress!

"Will it be okay?" Onward to therapy for ADHD

In summary, we miss the point when we address only the typically considered triad of inattention, impulsivity, and hyperactivity. These symptoms are only the tip of the iceberg. Much greater problems have usually been plaguing the family, but often no one has understood that the associated symptoms described above are part and parcel of the same neurologically-based condition. Without this recognition, families have thought that their ADHD child also was "incidentally" uncooperative and apparently self-absorbed. Unless we recognize that these extended symptoms are typically part of the same spectrum, parents will not mention them, and doctors will never deal with them.

Given all of this, it is reasonable to ask, "Will this go away?" Personally, I would rephrase the question as, "Will it be okay?" The answer can be "yes," but we must recognize that this is often the "50-year plan." In other words, these children can be wonderfully successful adults, while they continue to work on these issues over their lifetime. Meanwhile, we "just" need to patiently steer them in the right direction by keeping it positive, keeping it calm, keeping it organized; and, possibly, adding medication. That is what the rest of this book is all about.

Finally, we must also keep in mind that some of the iceberg is fantastic and enviable. While the rest of us are obsessing about the future, or morosing about the past, people with ADHD are experiencing the present. ADHDers do smell the roses. (Unfortunately, they may be driving a car at the same time.) ADHDers can be a lot of fun. Dullness is never a problem. Their "why not?" attitude may free them to take chances that the rest of us may be afraid to take. Their flux of ideas may lead to creative innovations. Most importantly, their extreme passion can be a source of inspiration and accomplishment to the benefit of us all.

It's going to be quite a ride. Let's start by taking a practice quick quiz on executive functions. Take the quiz: it's quite a bit of fun, a great review, and a preview of what is coming up.

Pop quiz on executive functions

This entertaining open book quiz is designed to test and reinforce your understanding of ADHD. The answers are at the end of the quiz. Questions 1–5 relate to the following *true* story:

> *A 13-year-old boy with ADHD discovers that his orthodontic bite-plate is missing from its handy container. He angrily accuses everyone else of having taken it. His mother explains the blatantly obvious fact that no one else would be interested in his used dental appliance. He continues screaming and blaming her for its absence.*

1. This child is demonstrating good executive function in the areas of problem solving and frustration tolerance.

   (a) True.

   (b) False.

2. The accusatory behavior of this otherwise bright child can best be explained by:

   (a) He's not quite smart enough to comprehend that his bite-plate isn't worth stealing.

   (b) He's overwhelmed by frustration and is poor at calmly solving problems.

3. Yelling back and accusing your child of behaving horribly would:

   (a) Prompt him to say, "Oh, thanks for helping me see the error of my ways."

   (b) Cause him to be even further overwhelmed.

4. An initial attempt at helping him find the bite-plate is unsuccessful. A useful parental response at this point would be:

   (a) Keep escalating the screaming match.

(b) Stop, walk away, retain your composure, and resist the urge to get in the last word. Resume discussion when everyone is calm.

5. This type of outrageous behavior in your ADHD child:

(a) Is a common part of the brakeless behavior and poor problem solving we summarize with the letters ADHD.

(b) Is the result of a nasty and selfish child.

6. ADHD is primarily a disorder of:

(a) Inattention.

(b) Inhibition of anything but the present stimulus or thought.

7. Your child with ADHD plays guitar all afternoon, rather than complete her college applications. You can understand this behavior by realizing that:

(a) She'd secretly rather stay at home with you for another four years rather than go to college.

(b) Life with ADHD means life right now, in the present. It's not that she doesn't care about college. Rather, amazingly enough, this future event doesn't even show up on today's radar screen.

8. Executive functions include all except the following:

(a) Ability to recall—and thus learn from—the past.

(b) Ability to read well.

(c) Ability to anticipate and plan for the future.

(d) Ability to control frustrations.

9. Your goal as parent is to:

(a) Further inflame your child's overwhelmed state, leading to a deteriorating relationship.

(b) See your role as therapist—teaching her to *stop* and defuse the situation.

10. Extra credit questions:

   (a) Answer Steven Covey's question: What do you want your child to say about you at your eulogy?

   (b) What kind of nursing home do you want your child to choose for you?

Answers:

Questions 1–4 and 6–9: (b). Question 5: (a).

Chapter 2

Rule #1: Keep It Positive

Bad and good news

First, the bad news: kids with ADHD have lots of problems besides a short attention span. In fact, we just filled the entire previous chapter simply naming them all. Many of these difficulties affect not just the child, but spill over to affect everyone around him or her. If we want to maximize our child's chance for a successful future—and avoid our own institutionalization—we had better learn some behavioral approaches to ADHD.

Now, the good news: there are truly effective (albeit not instantaneous) ways to improve the lives of the ADHD child and her caregivers. These approaches can be simplified into four basic principles, each of which is based on the executive function explanation of ADHD:

1. Keep it positive.

2. Keep it calm.

3. Keep it organized.

4. Keep it going (i.e., keep doing 1 to 3).

Each of these basic principles is discussed in its own chapter, starting here with "keep it positive." The chapters on keeping it positive and keeping it calm are written largely from the perspective of the home environment; and the chapter on keeping it organized is written mainly from the school perspective. Of course, there is significant overlap. The works of Barkley

(2000), Greene (2005), Phelan (1994), Zeigler Dendy (2006), and others inspire many of these guidelines.

Keep it positive

Keep it positive. How does that help deal with the underlying executive dysfunction in ADHD? Remember that ADHDers are like moths drawn to the brightest light—unable to inhibit anything but the most attractive stimulus. Positive reinforcers make very attractive bright lights. After all, that's why we call them "positive" in the first place—because we naturally seek them out. Since much of human activity (such as doing homework or cleaning up your room) is not a very attractive task, then we may need to provide a trail of artificial bright (positive) lights to keep ADHDers moving in the right direction.

So, Rule #1 is to keep it positive. It seems obvious enough. After all, it is the rare person whose attitude is improved by constant criticism. Yet after years of frustration and unmet expectations, family relationships may have deteriorated to a life of sarcasm, putdowns, and arguments. Families may need some specific mindsets and techniques to get things on an upswing. Here they are.

Get "a kick" out of your child

At this point in your life, enjoying your child may seem like a long-lost idea. It's okay to be a little (or a lot) frustrated, as long as you still get "a kick" out of your child's unique qualities. Maintain a sense of humor! Laugh with each other! Celebrate the child's humor, creativity, passion, and "why not?" attitude! Seek to enjoy, not to be frustrated! It's never too late to let your child make you smile, even if you're just chuckling warmly in disbelief. These are amazing kids, even if they don't quite fit the mold of most people on planet Earth.

Let the child know that you believe in him or her, despite the difficulties. In her autobiography, Liane Holliday Willey (1999) explains: "The people who have proven that they will stand by me no matter what I say, think or do, have given me a finer gift than they will ever realize." This principle is so important that it bears repeating: *Get a kick out of your child!*

Use positive reinforcement when possible

Instead of negatively reinforcing wrong behavior, Dr. Barkley (2000) reminds us to set a reward for the correct behavior you would rather replace it with. For example, suppose that you are trying to correct a child's nasty behavior towards his sister. Your goal is that he should be nice to her. So, rather than punishing a child for yelling at his sister, reward him for each kind comment. Rewards should be immediate, frequent, powerful, clearly defined, preferably relevant, and consistent. Remember, only positive rewards will change behavior and improve attitude.

Keep it positive by redirecting before the problem occurs

When things start going badly, redirect to a positive direction rather than criticizing the misbehavior after it has already occurred. For example, if the child is just beginning to fight with her sister, then redirect/distract to a new activity, rather than hand out a punishment after the indiscretion. In this way, you might replace an afternoon of screaming with a trip to the ice cream parlor.

Seek first to understand, then react

It would be much easier to view a child positively if we could understand what underlies a child's actions. Understanding leads to empathy, and empathy is an antidote to anger. Unfortunately, we are usually so wrapped up in our own reaction to something that we never stop to ask, "What underlying factors made my fellow human being do that to me?" Usually, there's a good answer if we seek it out. Pausing to understand the reasons why others treat us as they do can help us control our impulsive responses. This is hard enough for us to do ourselves, no less for the brakeless ADHDer's who are entrusted to our care. Let's teach and model for our children: first, pause to understand. Then, react.

Ways to figure out why he behaved in that manner

Ask yourself, "Why did he do that?" There is always a reason, even if it does not appear rational, even if it causes the child to be shooting himself in his own foot, and even if the child himself is not aware of the reason for his behavior. There are several ways to gain insight into a child's behavior:

☐ Ask your child! You could always ask your child why he did something, and you could actually pay attention to and legitimize his answer. Let him know that you really heard by rephrasing what he said before you respond. Your child might be shocked that you are actually listening, and modeling this technique for your child might actually teach him to rephrase what he has heard before responding. This technique, called "reflective listening," avoids speculation, which can be frequently wrong. Be aware that some children might answer, "I don't know why I did that." They are probably telling the truth.

☐ Watch the child's reaction. We can gain a big clue into someone's reactions simply by observing it. Unfortunately, many people dismiss others as "overreacting." People do not overreact; people over-feel. When a child blows up over what seems like a trivial issue to us, it may help us to understand that in our child's mind this issue must have a tremendous amount of meaning. For example, imagine an ADHD child's tearful screaming over the process of getting dressed. He's not overreacting. He is living through a tough morning. Maybe that realization would change our reaction to his behavior. Children's "overreactions" are a window into the turmoil embroiling their minds.

☐ Ask yourself how you would feel in that situation. By simulating the situation on our own brain, we can get a rough idea of what someone else is likely to be feeling. However, remember that other people may approach a situation with different neurological wiring and "baggage" than we do, and may actually react differently.

☐ Remember that we are seeing only a part of what is going on in a child's life. By the time a kid with issues shows up in class, who knows what has gone on already that morning or the previous evening at home? Waking up and getting dressed may have been major fights. Homework may have been hours of frustration for everyone. And when the child comes home, the parent needs to remember that their special child may have had an especially difficult time at school.

□   The Four-Second Rule explanation. Often, the behaviors make sense if we remember that ADHD children live almost exclusively in the present without much ability for foresight. Remember: you can usually predict an ADHD child's actions by applying the Four-Second Rule and asking, "What would I do now if the world were going to end in four seconds?" If the world were going to end in four seconds, would you do your homework? Honestly, now. With such a mindset, choosing to play Nintendo right now actually is both understandable and predictable.

It is much easier to keep a positive attitude if you can use the above techniques to truly understand/empathize with your child. Only once you have actually stopped to understand is it then time to react.

Maintain a disability outlook

Perhaps oddly enough, considering your child as having a disability is a way to keep things positive. If you insist that there is no disability in self-control, then you are likely to conclude that your child is willfully disobedient. If you insist that your child has no problem with organization and foresight, then you will conclude that your child chooses to simply not care.

However, the good news is that these problems are nobody's fault. Not your child's, not yours. Indeed, the key to addressing these symptoms is to adopt what Barkley (2000) calls a "disability perspective." The difficulties of ADHD are true disabilities. These symptoms happen to the ADHD person, as much as they happen to the people around them. No one chose to have these problems. Hate ADHD, not the person with it. There are several reasons why it is hard to accept these undesirable behaviors as "real" disabilities:

☐ Unlike blindness or deafness, there is no external marker for these disabilities. As an example, consider a child who is blind and has ADHD. No one would ever think of punishing or yelling at the child for his physically obvious vision problem. Nor would they think that punishing the child for poor vision would in anyway help the situation. That would be blatantly ridiculous and unfair. Yet, when the same child overreacts or is disorganized as part of his ADHD, the lack of a physical marker for the ADHDers problem makes it much harder to empathically accept those difficulties as innate disabilities.

☐ Unlike physical disabilities, these personality problems often get directed against the caregiver. The deaf child, for example, is having difficulties but is not attacking us. Her problems evoke from us an instinct to aid her. In contrast, the ADHD child may yell or curse at the parent who is merely trying to help. In short, ADHDers are often not acting in an easily lovable way. No wonder that these disabilities are harder to accept.

☐ When our child acts up, the rest of society—along with us—tends to think of bad parenting as being the problem. As the child pulls candy off of the rack at the supermarket checkout line, we are sure everyone else is thinking, "Why can't you control that child? What is wrong with you!?" That feeling, in turn, leads to parental resentment aimed at the child. As we have seen, bad parenting does not usually cause ADHD.

☐ To accept that some people have a physiological reason for difficulty controlling their behavior runs counter to our deep convictions about who we are. Our society feels that we are in charge of our own "personality," or "will," or "soul." It is hard for us to accept that so much of ourselves is so heavily under the influence of neurotransmitters over which we may have little direct biological choice.

A disability outlook is not as much "fun" as just considering ADHDers as unique individuals with special traits. However, while we do need to celebrate their differences as much as possible, the disability outlook helps keep our reaction empathic and positive.

Minimize frustrations by taking a realistic look at the child you get every day

A realistic assessment of your child's starting point helps minimize your anger and frustration when she doesn't live up to what you would like. Periodically, take stock of who is showing up in your life everyday. This is your starting point. This is what you can likely expect today. Not a typical child. Once teachers and parents accept this starting point (which I assure you the child does not exactly want either), it is easier not to take everything so personally. Anger on the caregiver's part is reduced, since anger arises when there is discrepancy between what you expect versus what you get. We are simply dealing with the hand we've been dealt. It serves us well to think of special needs kids as "works in progress."

Don't take the difficult behaviors as personal affronts

The answer to the question, "Why can't he be like all of the other children?" is that he can't. It isn't personal. You just happen to be the person in the room. Parents need to see themselves as "therapists" for their problematic child—not as victims of him. Always remember that there is a real, live child underneath all of those problems.

It may also help to remember that the person who suffers most from these behaviors is usually the child himself. These children "shoot *themselves* in the foot" at least as often as they bother anyone else. What further evidence could we have that these problems are not fully within their control?

Forgive yourself daily

Dr. Barkley (2000) urges his readers to forgive themselves nightly for their inability to be perfect. Each night, review how you've done that day and how you could do it better. Then, remember that each of us is only human, and forgive yourself for these past imperfections. Keeping an understanding, forgiving, and positive attitude applies not only to the child, but to yourself as well.

Keep your relational bank account in the positive

It may help to consider that you have a bank account of experiences with the child: there are good times and bad times that can be deposited into your relationship. Your goal is to have the overall balance be in the positive. As you enter into each interaction, ask yourself, "Will my next comment/action make my bank account with the child run into debt or into a positive flow?"

Make sure that you take the good times with the bad. When she is finally ready to apologize, talk, or cuddle, then take her up on her offer right then and there. Your goal is to put some good times into your relationship. Take them as they come. Otherwise, you end up only with the bad.

Don't be a nasty cop

Dr. Joseph Carver (2005) teaches discipline techniques by using the following highway patrol analogy. Imagine being pulled over by a policeman for making an illegal turn. The policeman approaches your window, hands you the ticket, and proceeds to insult you: "Don't you have any respect for the safety of yourself or others? Don't you care about anything? You are such a jerk! And, besides, your car looks really filthy! Why don't you clean it up?" What would you think about the policeman? Would you want to have dinner with him tonight? Would you want to give him a hug at bedtime? Moral of the story: as you hand out the punishment, skip the nasty attitude. The punishment is bad enough. The nasty attitude just breeds resentment.

Minimize arguments with the "no-fault" approach

Zeigler Dendy (2006) has the very useful suggestion that rules be enforced with a no-fault approach. In other words, avoid arguments based on whose fault it is. Rather, just deal with the end results. For example, it doesn't matter why a child arrives home late. It doesn't matter that you forgot to remind her again about the time of her usual curfew. It doesn't matter that the cat ate her watch. It does not matter that the car ran out of gas. It does not matter that you didn't buy her a reliable car. She is late, this is the consequence, and this is the plan to prevent it from happening again. It really simplifies discussion, doesn't it? This approach is particularly useful for the majority of ADHD people who always blame others for their problems.

Could this sometimes be unfair? Sometimes, yes. But in the long run, arguments are diminished, and that is to everyone's advantage. A second important result of this approach is that it allows us to avoid direct criticism of the child. After all, we are not assigning blame to anyone. Thus, this approach is a rediscovery of the old adage, "Criticize the behavior, not the child."

Punishment is not your chance to inflict misery: it is your chance to improve your child's upcoming decisions

What is the purpose of punishment? Unless you are a sadist, you are not really trying to "get even" or to make little kids miserable. Rather, the purpose of a punishment presumably is to correct future behaviors. A modest, immediate punishment is likely to be at least as effective as a prolonged one. A spiral of increasing punishments is unlikely to work, and just saddles everyone with a prolonged period of unhappiness in the future. Consider the following scenario:

> Father: "If you don't apologize right now, you will be grounded tonight."
>
> Johnny curses.
>
> Father: "O.K. If you don't apologize right now, you'll be grounded this entire week."
>
> Johnny curses again. Soon, the punishment is up to being grounded for a month. There is still no apology, the child has a meltdown, and everybody is angry. Twenty-nine days pass of not seeing his friends. The family has been miserable.
>
> Child: "Dad, do you remember what I'm being punished for?"
>
> Father: "Johnny, I don't have a clue."

The punishment has far exceeded its usefulness, don't you think? So, when punishment is required, keep it immediate and controlled. Better yet, teach the skills needed to avoid the negative behavior in the first place—especially since punishment is not typically effective for children with ADHD. But that's the subject of problem solving. You'll have to wait for the next chapter for that.

Avoid the "resentment treadmill"

Resentment breeds resentment. Perhaps, the following sounds familiar:

> John is nasty to his mom. Mom stays quiet. John is nasty again. This time, Mom yells back. The next morning, Mom is still angry. She walks into the John's bedroom and starts in, "Why can't you even set your own alarm clock? After how you treated me yesterday, you still expect me to wake you up?" John is bewildered. He curses at his mother. John goes to school, acts disrespectfully (again); and gets in trouble with the teacher, who is still sensitized from yesterday's unpleasant classroom interaction.

Good morning. It's another day on the resentment treadmill.

By the time someone is reading this chapter, the resentment treadmill may have been running at high speed for some time. Each "side" (child or caregivers) can recite a litany of truly legitimate complaints against the other. The cycle leads nowhere good. Everyone can agree to that. Who is going to get off the treadmill first? Hint: it isn't going to be the dysfunctional child. That leaves the mature adult to take the first leap. That's you. Don't expect instant results or gratitude. It's all easier said than done: resentment and anger can be quite addicting.

If it's not actually useful, don't do it

An interaction between you and your child can fall into one of three categories: (a) useful; (b) useless; or (c) counterproductive. Actually, there is no such thing as the "useless" category. All useless interventions actually fall eventually into counterproductive, because they just lead to further frustration all around—making the next interaction even less likely to be helpful. Sometimes, relationships are at the point when a simple, "Hello, how are you?" consistently provokes an irritated response. So, if the question is not useful, don't ask it. At these times, Phelan (1994) suggests that if you don't have anything really nice to say (e.g., "Here's five bucks just because I feel like it."), then stay quiet.

Amazingly, many of us keep using the same "useless" or harmful strategies over and over again, as if they might magically work on the four hundred and first try. If asking the child to clean up his room has not worked for 12 years, it probably won't be effective today. An ineffective command or an unproductive chide:

- won't make the room clean

- won't improve your child's life

- won't improve her relationship with you.

So why do it? Seriously. Think about it. (So what should you do? See Collaborative Problem Solving, p.74.)

Avoid the "four cardinal sins"

Thomas Phelan (2004) identifies the "Four Cardinal Sins." These "sins" are ineffective and actually harmful. Why would we use them?

1. Don't nag. It hasn't worked yet. If you don't have anything nice to say, don't say it. Even simple comments like "How was your day?" may cause frustration in your child.

2. Don't lecture. It doesn't work either. Plus, given their sense of time, ADHDers will find the experience interminable. Instead, give one or two brief, clear instructions.

3. Don't argue. It takes two to fight. You cannot be involved in an argument unless you agree to join it.

4. Don't offer unscheduled, spontaneous "advice." What are the odds that your Nintendo playing teen will respond pleasantly to your request to discuss right now that book report which is due in several weeks? "Insight transplants" from you to your child, as Phelan calls them, are unlikely to work.

Instead, either decide that the issue is aggravating but not significant enough to warrant intervention (i.e., stay quiet); or, make an appointment with your child to discuss the issue.

Take steps to avoid lying

Half of the children with ADHD have a problem with lying (Barkley *et al.* 1990). Why? We don't exactly know, but here is my theory. Lying may occur because the child is totally befuddled as to how he got into this mess. There simply is no logical explanation (ADHD is not logical), but the world insists that the ADHDers come up with a logical explanation, so they make something up. Observing the unbelievable mental contortions of these children as they muddle through a lie provides a valuable window into their remarkable lack of problem-solving skills. Fortunately, lying seems to typically get better over the long run (see the pop quiz on lying at the end of this chapter). So, how do we work to prevent lying?

- Don't set them up to lie. If you already know about an infringement, just state the facts that you know, and proceed with the consequences using the "no fault" rule. Do not use this as an honesty test.

- Minimize the need to lie by eliminating punishments that are so severe that the child lies to avoid them.

- Develop a plan to solve the original problem area that led to the lie.

Behavioral reward systems

Remember, kids with ADHD are drawn to the brightest light. Rarely is a household chore a very bright light. So we can use artificial bright lights (called "positive rewards") to help keep kids with ADHD moving down an otherwise less-than-intriguing path.

Reward systems rely on children's natural desire to please their parents. If a child's basic relationship with her parents is so full of anger and resentment that she no longer finds pride in pleasing her parents, then those basic relationships need some healing first, before behavioral modification programs are likely to be successful (Barkley 2000). Set aside a period of special time (up to 30 minutes) where the goal is simply to exist together pleasantly in the same room. The child gets to choose the (reasonable) activity, and the parent gets to enjoy being near their child without provoking a world war. Avoid saying anything critical—even if it would be helpful. Keep questions and comments (even positive ones) to a minimal level. After all, interruptions are still annoying. The goal here is to put your account of good/bad interactions into a positive balance, making it more likely for the child to want to please you. That sets the stage for smoother discipline setting in the future. Dr. David Rabiner (2006) and Dr. Russell Barkley (2000) provide a full explanation of reward-based techniques.

Remember that some of the difficult child/adolescent behavior is simply normal

Around 8 to 12 years of age, even typical children may start to act negatively to adult intervention, and even typical teens go through a period where their respect for adult authority is less than maximal. All children and adolescents are still literally in the midst of a multi-year frontal lobe remodeling project. Does it really matter whether their frontal lobe dysfunction is due to their ADHD or to their ongoing construction plan? In either case, the brains didn't choose to be somewhat dysfunctional, and we need to slow down as we approach this ongoing worksite.

Thus, although we may be quick to pin all difficult moments with the child as being due to some "disorder," life with any child is never totally smooth. Indeed, there may even be an evolutionary reason that human children become annoying as teens: a learning specialist once pointed out (only half-jokingly) that if teenagers didn't get obnoxious, their parents would never be able to let their "babies" leave the house and start their own families (Barbara Stern, personal communication 2004). It may be comforting to know that every family up and down the street, and every teacher up and down the hallway, is having some problems as well. After all, misery loves company.

Review this text, and others, periodically

Nobody can keep all of this stuff in mind, and over time different strategies will need to be called into play. Review this text from time to time. Also, sign up for some of the email newsletters (listed in Appendix 3) to get periodic reminders and suggestions.

Top principles of ADHD management

1. Keep a sense of humor. Get "a kick" out of the kid. Seek to enjoy, not to scream.

2. Celebrate the ADHD person's humor, creativity, and passion. Hate ADHD, not the person with it.

3. Kids with ADHD will either require ongoing support before they mess up, or negative rewards after they mess up. Which kind of help do you want to provide?

4. You do not have a standard child. You can view the issue as a disability. Or, you can view it as wonderful uniqueness. Or, you can view it as both. The perspective of "standard," though, is not an option.

5. Recognize that attention issues in the child are only the tip of the iceberg that the whole family must address.

6. The "patient" in ADHD is the whole family.

7. Instead of punishing wrong behavior, set a reward for the correct behavior you would rather replace it with. Rewards should be immediate, frequent, powerful, clearly defined, and consistent.

8. Plan ahead. Give warnings before transitions. Discuss in advance what is expected. Have the child repeat out loud the terms he just agreed to.

9. Don't argue, nag, or attempt unsolicited and spontaneous transplants of your wisdom to your child. Instead, either (a) decide that the issue is aggravating but not significant enough to warrant intervention; or (b) make an appointment with your child to discuss the issue.

10. Although it is not the child's "fault," he will still ultimately be the one to deal with the consequences of his behavior.

11. This is hard work.

12. You will make it through this. You have no other choice.

13. "The children who need love the most will always ask for it in the most unloving ways." (Words of a teacher quoted by Russell Barkley.)

14. If it is working, keep doing it. If not, do something else.

15. Forgive your child and yourself nightly. You didn't ask to live with the effects of ADHD any more than did your child.

16. Review this text, and others, periodically. You are going to forget this stuff, and different principles will likely be needed at different stages.

17. Steven Covey (2000) suggests imagining your child delivering your eulogy. What do you want him to say about you? Keep those bigger goals in mind as you choose your interactions/reactions to your child.

18. This is not a contest with your child. The winner is not the one with more points. The winner is the one whose child still loves them when they graduate from high school.

The chances for success are good

Your child's frontal lobes have another growth spurt in young adulthood. That fact, along with the skills we teach them, means that the chances for success are good—especially for children with higher socio-economic status, higher intelligence, better early peer relations, less aggression, less psychopathology in the parents, and less conflict with their parents. We can't solve all of the problems at once. Stay calm. She'll probably get into college even if today's English homework is late. Have some fun. And remember that your endpoint is not just your child's academic and social success—it also includes a good relationship with you.

Pop quiz on lying

This quiz is based on the following true story.

Jack, a 15-year-old boy with ADHD, does all of his homework on a laptop because of his horrific handwriting. His parents cleverly set the rule that no games are allowed on that computer. One night, Mom detects that it has been too quiet for too long in Jack's room. She sends Dad in to check. Dad opens Jack's door, at which point Jack immediately slams shut the laptop lid. Dad asks to look over the computer to see if any games have mysteriously loaded themselves onto it. Jack grabs the computer, runs into the basement and locks the door. Ten minutes later, he comes out—announcing that Dad can now check the machine. Dad, computer whiz that he is, checks the "Recycle Bin" and finds that the "Lord of the Rings" video game was deleted at 8:51 pm. The little clock at the bottom right corner of the laptop screen reads 8:52 pm. Dad points this out to Jack.

1. Teens can be trusted to use their laptops for only educational purposes.

   (a) True.

   (b) False.

2. Regardless, the parents were appropriate to allow their child to use a laptop to accommodate his dysgraphia and spelling problem.

   (a) True.

   (b) False.

3. Jack apparently doesn't think that Dad will find his son's running downstairs in order to lock himself in the basement as being suspicious behavior. In this regard, Jack demonstrates good executive function in the area of stopping long enough to think about how his actions appear to others.

   (a) True.

   (b) False.

The saga continues. Dad says, "Look, Jack. Bill Gates from Microsoft just documented that a video game was deleted at 8:51—while you were locked in the basement alone with your laptop—and it's now 8:52. Let's just practice honesty. Tell me that you deleted the game and I will grant you total amnesty. Of course, the game will stay deleted, but there will be no punishment or even any lectures. Let's just practice honesty, so that I can trust you next time... Did you delete the program?" Jack replies, "No!"

4. Given the overwhelming damning evidence against it, a typically functioning brain would have taken Dad up on the offer of amnesty. Anything else would be "shooting yourself" in the foot.

(a) True.

(b) False.

5. Any brain that refuses to take such a generous offer must be suffering from some sort of glitch.

   (a) True.

   (b) False.

6. This glitch can be thought of as a problem with executive function in the areas of problem solving ("How do I get out of this mess?") and foresight ("What's the best way to salvage my future trustworthiness and reputation?").

   (a) True.

   (b) False.

7. Kids with ADHD are poor at the executive functions of problem solving and thinking about the future.

   (a) True.

   (b) False.

8. Jack's lies are:

   (a) "evil" and deliberately deceptive.

   (b) clumsy, short-sighted and self-defeating.

9. Most likely, Jack does not have even the faintest idea why he lied.

   (a) True.

   (b) False.

10. Since Jack's lie was due to an ongoing disability in executive function, punishing Jack for his behavior is likely to change his behavior next time.

    (a) True.

    (b) False.

11. Punishing Jack for his behavior is likely to improve his attitude or his relationship with you.

    (a) True.

    (b) False.

12. It makes sense to hand out a major punishment for this behavior.

    (a) True.

    (b) False.

13. Better approaches would include:

    (a) Working cooperatively with Jack in advance to avoid the problem (e.g., allowing more time on the family computer that does have games on it).

    (b) Avoiding setting Jack up to fail the "honesty test." Instead, tell Jack that you know he deleted a game, instead of asking him about it.

    (c) Using the "no-fault" approach, state, "A game ended up on your computer and this is the following predetermined modest consequence." Lying to avoid responsibility is minimized if no one is assigning responsibility.

    (d) Be sure that Jack knows in advance that the punishment will not be so horrible that he needs to lie in order to avoid it.

    (e) All of the above.

Answers:

1. (b), 2. (a), 3. (b), 4. (a), 5. (a), 6. (a), 7. (a), 8. (b), 9. (a), 10. (b), 11. (b), 12. (b), 13. (e).

Chapter 3

Rule #2: Keep It Calm

Johnny is upstairs in his room working on his physics homework. Yes, working on his physics homework all by himself! Mom calls out cheerfully, "Johnny, come to dinner! I made you your favorite meal!" Johnny screams back, "No! Go away! Leave me alone!"

People don't think clearly when they are overwhelmed

What's going on in the vignette above? Johnny's negative response clearly has nothing to do with the actual request. After all, it's not that the physics homework is that much fun. (It's not like he's being called away from a videogame.) And it's not like he's being called to do anything so terrible. After all, his mom has made him his own favorite dinner. (Heaven forbid that he should eat what everyone else is having.) All he has to do is come and eat it.

Day after day, it's hard to fathom how Johnny could "choose" this counterproductive response. But that is just the point. Johnny isn't "choosing" anything. In fact, he isn't even thinking. When his nervous system is overwhelmed by frustration (in this case, due to a problem with the skill of "shifting agenda"), all that he can do is react. This is the executive function basis for Rule # 2: keep it calm. Since ADHDers are brakeless, then the first thing that we need to help them do is to put on the brakes—i.e., stay calm.

Major Rule #2: Keep it calm
Seek to defuse, not to inflame!

The life of a special needs child is overwhelming. The treatment for his overreaction is to defuse the situation, not to inflame it. This applies whether the child has ADHD, oppositional defiant disorder, bipolar depression, anxiety disorder, or just about any condition. Actually, this principle applies to just about any human interaction.

Seek to defuse, not to inflame. When tempers or anxieties flare, allow everyone to cool off. Remember, the caregiver may have to cool off as well. Serious discussion can only occur during times of composure. Negative behaviors usually occur because the child is spinning out of control, not because he is evil. Therefore, for "explosive" kids, the first step is to "*just stop!*" A defusing and problem-solving technique—labeled "Plan B" by Dr. Ross Greene (2005)—focuses on preventing overheated meltdowns. Preferably, we anticipate problems and try to head them off. We stop, we stay calm, and we negotiate if possible. The key to starting the whole process is to *stop and stay calm!*

"Just stop!" is the key

As described in Chapter 1, the primary difficulty in ADHD is a lack of inhibition of the present, thus making it difficult to use your other executive functions to plan the future. In other words, people with ADHD have trouble applying their brakes. They have trouble stopping, and nothing good comes from speeding out of control. So, the first step of treatment is to just *stop!* Once everyone stops, then time can cool our minds. Executive function can regain control. We can chart a productive course. Only once you have stopped at the corner of Calm and Calamity, can you then actually decide which way you want to proceed (see Figure 6).

There are several amazing things that come from just stopping (if you can do it):

1.   It works! Time heals. Even five or ten minutes is usually enough for the most brakeless ADHD brain to regain composure. If it routinely takes more than 30 minutes to return to a calm state, consider other diagnoses such as bipolar depression.

Figure 6: Welcome. You've stopped at the corner of Calm and Calamity. Now, you may choose which way you want to go

2. With the benefit of time to regain composure, most people will reach the right conclusion. They will begin to comply. If you just calmly state what is expected as you leave the scene of the impending argument, you will be typically surprised that—at some point fairly soon—the child is addressing the situation. Not always, but surprisingly often. After all, ADHDers are usually far from stupid. They know the rules of morality. They know the right thing to do. They just need a little longer than the rest of us to regain control and then sort it all out. A formal procedure for thinking through choices is described later this chapter.

3. Once you and the child have cooled down, the other behavioral methods will usually be quite clear. In other words, most of the advice in sections on behavioral management will seem almost blatantly obvious if you are calm. For example, we discuss keeping it positive. We discuss seeking to understand, and making the child part of the problem-solving process. We discuss choosing only productive punishments. When you are calm, these approaches are almost self-evident and not exactly rocket science. When you are screaming, these approaches are not available. In the heat of the moment, grounding the child for an entire year just might seem like a good idea.

Just stop! This means you, too

Yes, you. There is no one else reading this right now. I mean you. You have to put on the brakes as well. You are a human being who is struggling with self-control, also. Although your brain theoretically has normal control, ADHD in the family can be so exacerbating and even demoralizing that our ability to stop and see things clearly is debilitated as well. Note that there is a 40% chance that one of the parents of an ADHD child also has ADHD—so, indeed, there may be biological reasons why stopping is so hard in these families.

Why would we expect the child to be the only one trying to exert self-control? Why would we expect the one with a recognized physiological disability in self-control to be the only one working on the project?

How about ourselves? You may answer, "Well, I'm so overwhelmed and stressed by my environment that it's hard to stay in control. All of my buttons have been pushed." Welcome to the club. That's what your child is experiencing, also. You won't let him get away with that excuse.

Screaming at the child actually makes it harder for him to regain self-control

He is already overwhelmed. He is already overloaded and overstimulated. The last thing he needs is more stress. Being screamed at just inflames the situation, and ultimately makes it harder for your child to regain the executive functions needed to reach the right decision (see Figure 7). Further

Figure 7: Being yelled at does not help an ADHD brain

stressing an already overwhelmed nervous system is likely to result in a meltdown.

Warning symptoms of getting overheated: the stress gauge

The earliest signs of impending meltdown include raised voices, tightened muscles, reddened faces, or grunting noises. Time to defuse is running out. But at this point you may be able to salvage the situation with humor, negotiation, redirection of the conversation, maybe even a few deep breaths, or shutting up.

A little later, the signs of being overwhelmed get even more obvious, if we would just listen. They are usually something subtle like, "STOP! Get out! Leave me alone! I can't take it, anymore!" Your child is not making this stuff up. That is how he feels. Pretty awful. Take his advice. Stop. He is actually telling you in clear words just what you need to know: "I need to stop, now!" Ideally, he would have said it calmly. Ideally.

It may help to consider a stress gauge to help determine your child's and your own stress levels (see Figure 8). At 0 miles per hour (mph),

Figure 8: The Stress Gauge

everything is calm. Keep working with your child. At 10–20 mph, you're missing the mark, but he's still calm enough to keep at it. At 30 mph it is actually your last chance to back off, because at 40–50 mph, he's already been pushed over the cliff and is at the point of no return to that big meltdown of 60 mph. So, the goal is to back off at 30 mph, rather than waiting until you hit the point of no return! The goal is to stop pushing at 30 mph. Once you reach 40–50 mph, a counterproductive meltdown is inevitable.

This is not the time to give in to our impulse to just get it over with. You might have the self-control to do that. Your ADHD child was not born that way. Don't assume that he can handle it, just because you can. All brains have equal rights, but all brains are not constructed the same.

"But what if he doesn't just stop?"

Encourage compliance with the system by ensuring that the child recognizes that this cooling off period is not punishment. It is not like the old punitive "time out" in the corner system, which works best with elementary school age students. Rather, the child gets to do some pleasant—yet soothing—activity. Consider listening to music, playing Legos, or reading something of their choice. In general, avoid anything with a screen. Adrenaline producing activities such as Nintendo, playing on the computer, or watching television may be hard to stop after the intended five minutes. Do not forget a similar system for yourself.

If offering a pleasant activity doesn't work—and there are some children for whom it won't—then ignore the child. It takes two to fight. No one can enlist you in an argument unless you enter the arena.

After stopping, then state the rule once and leave

The decision to declare a cooling off period has nothing with who "won." First of all, this is not war. You are not trying to "win." Second, you are not giving in. Calmly state the rule or action that is required, and end the interaction. As you head down the hallway, ignore the ramblings of melted neurons. Come back later when cool heads prevail. That's when the discussion that actually counts will occur.

"But all he ever does is ask to stop. How do we ever get anything done?"

Good point. But, here are your choices:

1. Keep fighting for 30 minutes, get nothing accomplished, chip away at your relationship with your child, and increase household frustration levels thereby making the next blowup more likely.

2. Take a five- to ten-minute break, get something accomplished, maintain your relationship with your child, and lower household frustration levels making the next blowup less likely.

When you stop and think about it, the choice is pretty obvious, isn't it? Yet when faced with that choice in the heat of the moment, most of us have been taking the wrong course. Indeed, this is not always a terribly efficient system. However, neither you nor your child has been dealt great choices. Stopping, though, is the least bad option. It certainly beats the alternative of counterproductive screaming. You already know that does not work. Good luck, and do not expect results overnight. This is a multi-decade task to learn. Model it well. Once you've stopped, you are ready for the next steps.

The Collaborative Problem Solving approach

As we have seen, staying calm is essential to productive problem solving. Ross Greene beautifully builds upon this first step. The reader is strongly encouraged to read Dr. Greene's life-altering book, *The Explosive Child* (2005), that forms the basis of the following discussion of his Collaborative Problem Solving mindset and model. Let's take a closer look at his approach. (Adapted with the permission of the publisher and author.) It starts with Greene's mindset: "Kids do well if they can."

Kids do well if they can

Johnny wakes up in the morning, and ponders:

> "Gee, I could do all of my work today, get good grades, work towards getting into a good college, and have a nice career. I could control myself, have fun with my family, and get praises and hugs.

> Or, I could blow off all of my school work, get bad grades, be yelled at, blow up in a big explosion, and get punished.
>
> Hmm! Tough choice! You know, the one where I get in trouble sounds so inviting! Let's go for that one!"

Not. Do we really think that kids go through such a thought process of deliberately sabotaging their lives? When we think about it that way, it sounds pretty ridiculous. So if children are not choosing to have miserable lives, then we are left with the only other logical conclusion: ADHD kids don't act like everyone else because they can't—at least not with the skill set or environment they currently have right now.

So if a child isn't choosing to have a meltdown, what is causing it? Greene points out that certain kids lack important skills in the general areas of flexibility, frustration, and problem solving. A meltdown occurs when the demands being placed on such a child's brain outstrip the child's limited abilities to cope. At that point, the child is reduced to a blithering blob of neurons, incapable of anything more sophisticated than screaming. It's pretty sad, actually. Now, it would have been nice if the child could have just said, "Mom, I appreciate your point of view, but I really can't cope with this discussion right now. I am beginning to become frustrated and overwhelmed. Can we continue this conversation in fifteen minutes when I can think more clearly?" It would have been nice. And should the stressed child ever be so lucky as to actually put such feelings into words, it would have been nice if the parent would abide by that request. It would have been nice. Just not very likely, at least not without practice.

Greene's "pathways" to poor frustration tolerance and inflexibility

So, what skill deficiencies might lead a child to negative and explosive behaviors? Greene identifies five clusters of skills, or "pathways," that can set the stage for this "learning disability" in the areas of flexibility, frustration tolerance, and problem solving:

1. Executive function skills. As we have already seen in Chapter 1, executive function problems are built into the definition of ADHD. It is not surprising, then, that 80% of children

identified by Greene (2005, p.144) as "explosive" carry the diagnosis of ADHD. The most common executive function problems which set off outbursts are:

(a) Trouble shifting agendas. Shifting agendas at the whim of other people is a huge problem for ADHD kids. Here's a typical scenario. Mom says, "Billy, stop reading and take a shower." Billy screams back, "No!!!!!"

(b) Trouble with self-talk. It's hard to talk yourself through a problem if you have trouble talking to yourself. This leads to ADHDers getting "stuck" on one solution.

(c) Trouble with organization. It is difficult for ADHD kids to come up with more than one idea, or to organize their ideas as they try to solve problems.

(d) Trouble with hindsight/foresight. It's hard to solve problems successfully if you can't recall past successes/failures, or keep the big future picture in mind.

2. Language processing skills. Some children demonstrate such obvious speech or communication delays that they can be readily identified as having difficulty expressing their problems and frustrations. Without the ability to manipulate words to form complex thoughts, they may even have trouble clarifying the problems for themselves, no less trouble communicating them to others. However, even children with superficially normal language skills may be deficient in the basic vocabulary of emotions and needs. They may never have learned to actually use the phrase, "I'm frustrated!" rather than cursing. Some children do well with an emotion scale of 0–10, or a set of colors to describe the degree or type of emotion. If they already could have developed such skills on their own, they would probably have been using them by now.

3. Emotional regulation skills. Children with ADHD are brakeless. There is difficulty modulating the magnitude of the response to frustration. Little frustrations may truly feel like major disasters. In addition, many children have chronic

irritability, agitation, or anxiety issues that make it difficult to regulate their emotions so that they can think clearly.

4. Flexible thinking skills. Children with ADHD (and Asperger's as well), tend to see the world in an all-or-nothing, black-and-white fashion. Unfortunately for them, our world contains not only shades of gray, but also colors. For such a person, watch out when a black-and-white rule, routine, or expectation is violated.

5. Social skills. Some children may have trouble picking up social cues. Missing or misinterpreting the subtext of a situation is a recipe for a blowup. Such kids may have conditions such as autistic spectrum disorders, or ADHD. (In ADHD, the kids are capable of picking up social clues, but are too overwhelmed with other things to pay attention to them.)

Greene's specific "triggers" that overwhelm those pathways

Triggers are the specific events that unleash a trip down one of these inadequate skill pathways. Greene calls these "problems that have yet to be solved" (if the problems were already durably solved, they would not be causing meltdowns anymore!). Although it may seem that everything and anything sets your child off, there are usually just a handful or two of specific triggers that push a child over the edge. Some of the more common triggers include homework, homework, and homework. (A therapist once commented that if homework were eliminated in this country, she'd be out of a job.) Other common triggers include: switching activities according to someone else's agenda (such as to stop playing videogames now, or come to dinner now), the morning routine, and the bedtime routine.

Greene suggests starting by writing down the specific triggers over the next week that predictably cause difficulty between you and your child. Then start using Collaborative Problem Solving to resolve those problems so they don't set the stage for challenging behavior anymore. Remember:

- Triggers are "problems that have yet to be solved" (Greene 2005, p.47).

- Problems are "two concerns that are yet to be reconciled" (Greene 2005, p.104).

Handling triggers with plans A, B, and C

Dr. Greene describes three ways of handing a child's triggers: plans A, B, and C.

□ Plan A: The adult imposes his/her authority upon the child. It's the "I'm the parent, and you will do it my way or the highway" approach. Many of the standard reward/punishment/token systems are based on this method (see Silver 1999; Barkley 2005). Unfortunately, punishment does not teach needed skills or resolve problems durably—it hasn't yet, has it? Indeed, if you were lucky enough to have a child for whom this approach actually worked, you probably wouldn't be reading this chapter. Plan A causes meltdowns in kids with a learning disability in the domains of flexibility, frustration tolerance, and problem solving. Greene (p.78) puts it this way:

Inflexibility + Inflexibility = Explosion

□ Plan B: Stay calm and work out a mutually satisfactory and doable solution to the problem. Plan B comes in two varieties:

  ○ Emergency Plan B: where triggers are defused during the heat of the moment as passions are rising. Much less ideal.

  ○ Proactive Plan B: where triggers that overload skill sets are identified and solved collaboratively (together) in advance. Because meltdowns are highly predictable—once you've identified the problems that are triggering them—then this is the form of Plan B you should be using most often.

□ Plan C: The parent decides that this issue is not worth pursuing at this point in time with this particular child. This is not "giving in." Giving in is starting with a demand in Plan A and switching mid-tantrum to Plan C. You are not giving up control when you decide to handle a problem with Plan C. You have decided which issues are to be worked on now, and which are better postponed. A common problem amenable to Plan C is keeping the child's room clean. Most likely, you've got bigger issues to deal with currently, so it might be appropriate to put the dirty-underwear-on-the-floor-debacle on hold. Importantly, if you do choose Plan C for this problem—and clean up the room yourself—be sure not to complain about it later. That would be the worst of all worlds: the child never practiced the skill, you had to do the work, and you still made him angry at you because of your complaints! How much sense does that make?

Plan B (Collaborative Problem Solving) in more detail

For Plan B to be effective, it is essential that everyone stays as calm as possible. Once again, that includes you. That's why Proactive Plan B is better than Emergency Plan B, the latter being invoked when things are already emotionally spiraling downhill. Greene's Plan B is also called Collaborative Problem Solving, and requires you to lend your own frontal lobe to your child as you guide him through the process—until it becomes second nature to the child or until his own frontal lobe grows new neural connections during young adulthood. There are three steps to Collaborative Problem Solving:

1. The child gets his concern on the table, and the adult expresses empathy for it.

2. The adult gets his concern on the table.

3. The child is invited to start the process of finding a doable, win–win solution to the concerns in Steps 1 and 2.

Let's look a little further at each step.

STEP 1: CHILD PUTS HIS CONCERN ON THE TABLE AND ADULT EXPRESSES EMPATHY

Note that here are two goals of Step 1: the kid gets his concern about a given problem out for discussion, and the kid is reassured of the adult's empathy for that concern. These two goals may actually proceed in either order. Sometimes, the child will be able to spontaneously articulate his or her concern, in which case the adult's response of empathy comes second.

This empathic response might be something simple, such as repeating what the child just said ("So you're angry that you didn't get to play videogames today.") or a simple, "I hear you." (Teenagers tend to respond better to the "I hear you.") Other times, the adult will need to start the process with an observation, in order to get the child to even recognize that there is an issue—no less to start talking about it. In this case, the adult might start out with, "I've noticed you've been cranky in the afternoons. What's up?"

During the empathy phase, the adult is not saying "yes" or "no," just that we are going to have a calm discussion about this. The empathy response helps keep everyone calm, and reassures the child that his concerns are not going to be blown off the table.

Many explosive children have trouble expressing themselves. After all, that may be the pathway that led to their explosive nature in the first place. (Remember: self-talk is not a strength for ADHDers.) Such a child's response to "What's making you cranky?" could be an honest, "I don't know." In that case, the adult might have to add a few educated guesses. These children may need to be taught how to stop long enough to recognize what's bothering them, and how to articulate these concerns and feelings. How do we teach that? Speech therapists can help teach basic vocabulary to some kids who never could or never did practice using terms before such as, "I'm happy," "I'm sad," "I'm angry," or the biggie, "I'm frustrated." Short of speech therapy, just practicing the steps of Collaborative Problem Solving is modeling/teaching the process. Offering the child some possible choices may help, such as, "Are you cranky because you are tired, because you are hungry, because you are angry at your sister, or because you don't have enough time for videogames?" With practice, the child is being shown how he can use his own words to identify the problem.

STEP 2: THE ADULT PUTS HIS CONCERN ON THE TABLE

In Step 2, the adult expresses his concern about the same problem. For example, "I hear that you are frustrated that you don't get enough time to play videogames, but let me tell you what I'm worried about. I'm afraid that when you keep staying up late at night playing games, then you are always tired the next day, which makes you cranky." Now, with both sides using calm words to express their points of view, we actually know what concerns we need to reconcile. The child doesn't need to really care about your feelings on the issue. Rather, he just needs to take them into account as you and he work towards a mutually satisfactory solution.

Interestingly, when the adult works to express her concern, she may find that she really doesn't have one! For example, the mother might realize that although she doesn't like the idea of videogames, the child is actually finishing all of his homework and getting to bed on time. In such a case, the problem is solved, because there really isn't any.

Also, note that Steps 1 and 2 involve putting concerns on the table, not solutions. For example, the adult should say, "I'm concerned that video games are interfering with your sleep" (stating a concern) rather than saying, "You should be asleep by 10 pm" (stating a solution). If the solution is already being presented, that's Plan A, and we never get to Step 3.

STEP 3: THE CHILD IS INVITED TO START SEEKING A WIN–WIN SOLUTION

In this last step, the adult invites the child to start exploring solutions that are both mutually satisfactory and actually doable. Try, "Let's work on this together. Any ideas?" Initially, the goal is to come up with as many solutions as possible. For the moment, praise them all. The child needs to meet with success as he starts the process. Later, we'll sort out which one would be best. Greene proposes that solution ideas come in three basic categories:

1. Ask for assistance.

2. Compromise.

3. Seek an "out-of-the-box" solution.

So, the child may benefit from being taught how to run through these different categories as he attempts to come up with solutions. Returning to the videogame example, the child's asking for assistance probably wouldn't work—no one else knows how to play the game as well as he does. How about a compromise: "I could play for up to one hour but only if I'm done by 10 pm." For an out-of-the-box solution, "How about if I wake up at 7 am on Saturday mornings and play for a few hours?"

Note that the solution agreed upon has to truly meet the needs of both sides—or it won't work. Also, the solution must be truly doable (by both the child and the adult). Otherwise, it is just an exercise in self-delusion. How do we know then a solution fails to meet these criteria? Simple. The solution doesn't work. It's time to start the process over again, or at least refine it. Don't see going back to the drawing board as a failure. At least you're teaching skills and working on the problem as a team. Disabilities are not cured overnight.

Collaborative Problem Solving teaches most of the deficient skills

As you see, this process models skills and actually teaches the child the skills that he is likely deficient in—rather than just counterproductively punishing him for not already having them. Learning the skills of Collaborative Problem Solving addresses many of the pathways to frustration. Some children will also benefit from speech therapy and/or social skills training and/or medication. A professional therapist can be of great help to the family in implementing this technique. And remember: many of these children will require decades of hands-on support at the time of need to actually execute these skills.

Pop quiz on keeping it calm: the "Sheetrock Index"

In my practice, I've developed the "Sheetrock Index," which is the number of times per semester that the child puts his fist, foot, or other body part through the sheetrock (drywall). The goal is to keep the Sheetrock Index at 0, but at least no higher than one per semester. If the child hits the wall but there is no actual hole, I'm sorry, but the child does not get any points. Consider the following hypothetical but fairly common scenario.

> *Ralph comes home after school. He's gotten some bad grades back, he's hungry, and he's not in that great a mood. Mom wants to chat.*
>
> *Mom: "How did you do on that social studies test we studied for?"*
>
> *Ralph: "Leave me alone."*
>
> *Mom: "You studied really hard for that test. I hope you did well."*

Ralph: "LEAVE ME ALONE!"

Mom: "I'm just asking!"

Ralph: "LEAVE ME ALONE! GET OFF MY CASE!!!

Mom: "Don't talk to me like that!"

Without warning, Ralph puts his fist through the sheetrock in the wall. Again. Mom cries. Again.

Answer the following questions, based on the above vignette:

1. Ralph is good at the executive function of frustration tolerance.

   (a) True.

   (b) False.

2. Ralph is good at the skill of using sophisticated words to express his feelings.

   (a) True.

   (b) False.

3. Mom is good at using the stress gauge.

   (a) True.

   (b) False.

4. Utilizing the stress gauge (and backing off when it was rising) would have been preferable to relying on the "Sheetrock Index."

   (a) True.

   (b) False.

5. This family could have used some Collaborative Problem Solving skills to avoid this totally unnecessary meltdown. For example, the team could have worked out in advance that there will be no "small talk" until after the afternoon snack has kicked in.

   (a) True.

   (b) False.

6. Dad comes home and finds bits of sheetrock all over the floor, and everyone in an angry mood. He starts yelling, again. This teaches Ralph how to calmly express his own frustration with words.

   (a) True.

   (b) False.

7. It's time to repair the sheetrock. This needs to be an activity filled with anger and resentment (as if that would help family dynamics).

   (a) True.

   (b) False.

8. Sheetrock repair can be a productive and bonding experience. Sheetrocking together allows:

   (a) Bonding time between parent and child.

   (b) Teaches organizational skills (such as planning what supplies to get from Home Depot™).

   (c) Teaches fine motor skills such as taping and sanding.

   (d) Teaches foresight, such as remembering to save leftover paint for touch-ups.

   (e) All of the above.

Answers:

1. (b), 2. (b), 3. (b), 4. (a), 5. (a), 6. (b), 7. (b), 8. (e).

Note: Sheetrock repair instructions can be found at www.home-improvement-abc.com and www.bobvila.com.

Chapter 4

Rule #3: Keep It Organized and Other School Treatments

In the previous two chapters, we discussed the major rules of home treatments: keep it positive, and keep it calm. Of course, those principles apply to the school arena as well. In this chapter, we'll focus on the major rule for school treatments—keep it organized—along with other academic recommendations. Of course, parents will need to participate also with these accommodations at home.

Disorganization is virtually built into the definition of ADHD

Organization is the holy grail for ADHDers, as virtually all people with ADHD are innately disorganized. In fact, if we rearrange as follows the diagnostic criteria for the inattentive type of ADHD, we see that five of the nine possible criteria are purely organizational. (See the author's italicization.) The other four symptoms relate to short attention and easy distractibility. You can't meet the required six criteria for ADHD unless you at least dip into the area of being innately disorganized. Conversely, if you are disorganized, you are already five-sixths of the way to meeting criteria for ADHD:

- fails to give close attention; makes careless mistakes

- difficulty sustaining attention

- does not seem to listen when spoken to directly
- easily distracted by extraneous stimuli
- **difficulty organizing tasks**
- **fails to follow through (not volitional or incapable)**
- **avoids tasks requiring sustained organization**
- **loses things needed for tasks**
- **often forgetful in daily activities.**

So, disorganization is an executive dysfunction that is literally built into the diagnosis of ADHD. This explains the need for Rule #3: keep it organized.

Don't confuse disorganization with "He doesn't care."

A child with ADHD might indeed fight with his parents for hours as he muddles through his homework, and then he actually forget to hand it in! Now, it would be logical enough to assume that if a child does not hand in his homework, then he doesn't care. It would be logical enough; it would just be wrong. Think about it. If I were really lazy, then I wouldn't have done the homework at all in the first place. However, if I had just spent hours suffering through homework, I'd be darn sure to hand it in—if for no other reason than so that I could get away with not doing tomorrow's homework.

No typically functioning mind would do painful work and not seek credit for it. So what is going on? ADHDers don't have typically functioning brains in the area of organization. Their brain may be extremely capable in the area of writing an English paper, for example, but extremely poor in the area of organization required to find it the next morning. This striking unevenness in skills is what makes the organizational problem a disability.

"Sink or swim" does not work for kids with disabilities

Before we can discuss the specifics of any school (or home) interventions, we must first overcome the biggest hurdle to helping these students: the "fear of coddling." Some caring adults are concerned that they might be doing harm to the child's future by helping him too much now. "How will he ever learn if I keep intervening? Rather, let him sink or swim. That'll teach him and get him ready for the real world."

However, "sink or swim" does not work with disabilities. We wouldn't tell a child with dyslexia, "We already went over 'b's and 'd's yesterday. Get it right today or you'll be punished!" So why would we tell a child with a disability in organization that he had better overcome his disability today or be punished? If punishment was going to work for this child, it should have been working a long time ago. And it didn't, and it won't. Why? Because, although they may be bright in other areas, these kids can't swim yet when left to their own organizational abilities. If they could, they would have. Do we really think that these kids choose to do poorly?

Remember, kids with ADHD have trouble executing the skills that they have learned. As Barkley (2000) puts it, they have trouble doing what they know, not trouble knowing what to do. For example, they already know that they should write down all of their assignments, and then hand them in on time. Go ahead. Ask them if that's news. I'll wait.

See! They do already know what to do! It's just that their poor executive function doesn't allow them to execute those skills. So, we need to provide a safety net by constantly supervising that they have used the organizational skills that we teach them. And we'll need to keep using it. The safety net won't hurt them. See Chapter 5.

Don't worry that we'll be making their lives too easy. Even with our understanding and support, these kids will still suffer more frustration and setbacks than the average student. We should only wish that our interventions would be so successful that ADHDers' lives will now be easier than everyone else's.

The five major components of an organizational system

Not surprisingly, then, accommodations for an ADHD child's disorganization need to be a major part of school plans for ADHD. There are five principle elements required to keep a student organized:

1. *An assignment pad.* Ah, our trusty old friend, the assignment pad. So basic. After all, unless the child has his assignments in writing, how is he going to reliably do them? How will the parents know what they are supposed to ensure gets done? Thus, in the beginning of the year, we dutifully equip each child with an assignment pad. If only it were actually used! But, alas, kids with ADHD often don't have the executive functions to know where the pad is located, no less to actually use it every day for every subject. This is where surrogate frontal lobes come in—harmlessly donated by the classroom teacher, skills teacher, and parents. Teachers, please come around and check that the ADHD students are actually writing down their assignments! Do not wait for the student to come to you for your initials. If they were organized enough to do that, they would not have needed this accommodation in the first place. If you double-check this step of writing homework down, the child will actually get to practice using this skill—and might actually internalize it over the next couple of years. In any case, checking is more productive and easier than dealing with the missed assignment. Other options for making sure the child is aware of the assignments include:

   ○ Make sure child and parent know about routine assignments (such as a spelling test every Wednesday).

   ○ Provide written handouts of the week's assignments.

   ○ Put assignments on the internet. How great is that!

   ○ Be sure each student has the phone numbers of some classmates he can call if a particular subject is left blank. (If there really is no homework assigned for a particular day, the child should record, "No homework." A blank space triggers a phone call to a classmate to check. Don't take the child's word that the blank space means "no assignment." In God we trust—all others need to write it down.)

2. *A monthly planner.* The assignment pad records not just projects which are due tomorrow, but also projects which are due well

into the future. Question: What happens to those future assignments once you turn the page, and how do you plan for the long-term projects? Answer: you record them on a monthly calendar. For example, if a book report is due in two weeks, have your child write it down on the monthly calendar. Then, work with the student to break down the project and record the due dates for the multiple steps involved in the project—such as when to obtain the book, read the book, write the rough draft, edit it, and hand in the report. Remember, time is very vague to someone with ADHD. Make it visually tangible with the monthly calendar. Here's the due date for the report, written down right here on the calendar, just 14 inches (two weeks) away. And look, there is a final exam due just one inch (one day) before that. Looks like things are getting pretty close together. Perhaps we should start getting ready now, since we can literally see that they are so bunched up later.

3. *A bi-fold folder* for all papers coming from school (left side) and for all papers going back to school (right side). Johnny comes home and Mom wants to help her child get organized, but the backpack is such a disaster that it should be condemned. Papers are anywhere in the dozen or so hiding places in his multiple binders—not to mention between or under them. The solution: a bi-fold folder that has two pockets. On the left side of the pocket goes every piece of paper that has the child's fingerprints on it from today. If Johnny has touched it, it goes there. Later, at home, the papers can be put into their proper place, under careful surrogate frontal lobe supervision, if needed. But at least everyone knows where to look for all of the papers: on the left side of the folder. Now, let's fast forward to tomorrow, when the teacher asks for the math homework. Johnny looks everywhere and can't find it. He gets an "F." The solution is simple. On the right pocket of the bi-fold go all papers that are due to be handed in tomorrow. When the math teacher asks for the homework, there is only one place it could possibly be—in that right pocket. And we know that it's there

because the parents' surrogate frontal lobes provided a double-check safety net the night before. Remember, this bi-fold gets taken to every class.

4. *A single binder (or two).* Many teachers feel that they are teaching organization by requiring their students to have two or three notebooks or folders for each subject. The presence of multiple hiding spaces for papers spells disaster for an ADHD child, no less for the vertebral columns of all children. A single binder—or perhaps one for the morning and one for the afternoon—would work a whole lot better for ADHD kids. Some kids prefer an accordion file, with the first two sections used for work going to and from school.

5. *Most importantly, frontal lobes to supervise* continued use of the above. Surrogate frontal lobes will be required for the next few (say, 50 or so?) years to ensure that the above stuff is actually used. The day that someone stops providing a safety net that the child is actually performing these steps will likely be the day that organization falls apart. One more time: kids with ADHD already know what to do, they just can't execute it this decade. Take away the "scaffolding" of support (Brown 2005), and they will likely falter. If the organizational support is working, keep doing it.

Convert assignment pads into time schedules

Each day, the child and parent (and/or skills teacher) should look over the daily assignment pad as well as the monthly calendar of upcoming commitments and assignments. Any scraps of paper with notes on them should be rounded up and added to the list.

Next, convert the daily and monthly assignments into a time schedule for today—a "To Do" list. Write out the times that you are going to actually accomplish today's tasks. This provides a reality check for what can and cannot be crammed into one day. Note that what you are planning to actually accomplish today may not correlate exactly with what is on today's assignment pad.

- Include time for eating, bathing, instant messaging, television, etc.

- Factor in time for unexpected delays—work taking too long, demands from parents, phone calls from friends, traffic jams, etc. The unexpected is to be expected.

- Adhere to the time schedule. This will help prevent taking diversions, since there is always an immediate deadline to meet.

  - Caregiver and child should go over this time schedule as soon as the child makes it (which should be when coming home from school or in resource class). Children with ADHD typically have poor estimates of how long events will take. They will need our advice. Making this time schedule will allow them to see how well their estimates work out.

Use resource room or a classroom aide to give ongoing skills support for classified children

Just teaching the skill a few dozen times to the ADHD student is not sufficient. After all, if it were sufficient, we would not still be considering these students for a skills program. Each day, the skills teacher:

- checks the assignment sheet

- reviews the monthly calendar

- reviews due dates

- reviews the plan for breaking down larger projects into steps

- reviews needed books

- checks for daily class notes for each subject

- provides appropriate information to the parents—the other part of the team.

Allow the child to expediently make up missed work

The suggestion that teachers allow ADHD students to expediently make up missed work is likely to ruffle more than a few feathers! Let's list the justifications for this suggestion:

- If we follow the organizational system above, there shouldn't be that much missed work, anyway. We are only talking about an occasional missed assignment.

- As we have seen, organization is a disability for ADHD kids. Punishing a child with ADHD for his organizational problem is as fair and productive as punishing a child for her dyslexia. Punishment does not teach skills or cure disabilities.

- If a major deduction for lateness were going to work, it would have been working already.

- Allowing expedient make up ensures that the child eventually does put in the work, and provides a better education (see Table 6).

Table 6 Whether or not to allow expedient make up of work. Is the choice really difficult?

Allow expedient make up of missed work	Don't allow expedient make up of missed work
Child does the work.	Child doesn't do the work.
Child "gets away" with nothing.	Child "gets away" with not doing the work.
Child learns the material.	Child doesn't learn the material.
Child gets good grades.	Child gets bad grades.

If deduction for lateness actually works to correct the problem, then keep doing it. If not, recognize the problem as a disability that is currently unable to be completely corrected. In such a case, the work does need to be completed, but it is not fair for a persistent organizational disability to cause excessive and demoralizing deductions. Instead, use one of two methods:

- Accept work handed in within one day of both student *and* direct parental notification of the missing assignment.

- Alternatively, a non-punitive school detention can be assigned, during which the child gets the work done, and it is then accepted.

Failing is 65, not 0

If, for some reason, it is necessary to give an "F" for incomplete work, remember that an F is 65, not 0. Trying to get a decent quarterly grade while averaging in a 0 or two is virtually impossible. For example, if a student gets four grades of 90 and just one 0, her new average is 72. Very demoralizing. A grade of 0 is excessive, does not change the ADHDer's future behavior, and is actually counterproductive. From a purely mathematical perspective, you would have to get five points of extra credit on 20 assignments to compensate for losing 100 points on a single missed one.

Similarly, if you really do need to take off some points for late or missing homework, do it in moderation. Doesn't taking off 10% or so get your point across to everyone?

Teacher/parent communication in "real-time" is essential

In order to provide the ADHD child with the necessary organizational safety net, it is essential that teachers stay in close contact with the parents and/or resource room teacher. Use phone calls. Use email. But stay in touch! Don't expect the ADHD child to be a reliable link in this communication chain between teachers and parents. Note that mid-term progress notes come too late to do anything with the information.

Appropriately handling missed work will help the parents greatly

Another huge benefit of these approaches is that it allows the parent to back off some. Without the fear of a major deduction for missed work, the parent does not have to micro-manage each and every assignment—scouring everything to find that occasional missed assignment. That degree of parental involvement is typically not well tolerated by a pre-teen or teen, especially one with the low frustration threshold of ADHD. If teachers won't do it for the kid, they can do it for their fellow adults.

ADHD accommodations other than organizational support

Although organizational support is likely to remain the most prominent need for ADHD students, a host of other accommodations might also be helpful. Many of these can be done with or without formal classification of the child.

- Learn about ADHD. Typically, teachers in the higher grades have a harder time "believing" in the condition of ADHD. After all, the older students no longer have the obvious physical marker of hyperactivity. The residual attention, organization and preparation problems, however, are frequently misinterpreted as lack of interest and motivation. The school special education staff should have materials for classroom teachers (also see Appendix 3).

- Look for associated problems. Of students with ADHD, 70% will have some sort of learning disability. Particularly common are poor handwriting (dysgraphia), poor expressive writing skills, poor spelling, poor following of directions, and poor following of a sequence of commands. Many also have reading, math, or processing disabilities as well. Besides academic difficulties, there may also be anxiety, depression, tics, sensory integration, or other issues. As shown in Chapter 1, these problems can frequently mimic, co-occur, or worsen each other.

- Don't take the ADHD behaviors as personal challenges. The answer to the question, "Why can't he listen to me like all of the other children?" is that he can't turn off his ADHD at will. It isn't personal.

- Take a realistic outlook at the child you get every day. Dr. Phelan (1994) suggests periodically rating the ADHD behaviors using a brief checklist. Here's a possible one:

- ○ Distractibility   _ _ _ _ _ _
- ○ Disorganization   _ _ _ _ _ _
- ○ Impulsivity   _ _ _ _ _ _
- ○ Hyperactivity   _ _ _ _ _ _
- ○ Over-feels   _ _ _ _ _ _
- ○ Socialization problems   _ _ _ _ _ _
- ○ Poor handwriting   _ _ _ _ _ _
- ○ Other   _ _ _ _ _ _

This is your starting point. Not a typical child. This is what you can likely expect from him every day. Once teachers and parents accept this starting point (which I assure you the child does not exactly want, either), it is easier not to take everything so personally. Also, anger on the caregiver's part is reduced—since anger arises when there is a discrepancy between what you expected versus what you got. The parents and teachers can both fill out the checklist, and discuss it with each other. They will realize that they are allies.

- ☐ Provide help for deficits at the moment it is needed, not negative feedback when it is already too late. As said previously, the simple reality is that punishment does not usually teach the needed behaviors to ADHD kids. This is because many children with ADHD have difficulty "doing what they know," not "knowing what to do." They already "know," for example, that they should come to class prepared. Once we understand that punishment has not been working, we are ready to provide relief for their disabilities by guiding them at the moment guidance is needed—rather than continued disbelief that they did it wrong again. Someone has to stay in the trenches with these kids.

- ☐ Present material to ADHD children in the following manner:

  - ○ Provide the child with "preferential" seating. Some students do better right next to the teacher. For others, being near the buzz of activity that surrounds the teacher is too distracting. These kids might do better in a quieter part of the classroom seating.

- ○ Present material in an animated fashion. Remember that kids with ADHD are like moths. They will pay attention to whatever is the brightest light. The teacher needs to be more interesting than the paperclip on the desk.

- ○ Establish good eye contact.

- ○ Tap on the desk (or use another code) to bring the child back into focus.

- ○ Alert the child's attention with phrases such as "This is important."

- ○ Alert children that they are about to be called on. This avoids the public embarrassment of being caught unprepared for the question.

- ○ Break down longer directions into simpler chunks.

- ○ Check for comprehension.

- ○ Encourage students to underline the key words of directions.

- ○ Encourage students to mark incorrect multiple-choice answers with an "x" first. This allows them to "get started" quickly, while forcing them to read all of the choices before making a final selection.

☐ Allow physically hyperactive children out of their seats to hand out and pick up papers, etc.

☐ Keep students and parents apprised of their grades. ADHD students often have an inflated sense of how well they are doing. A tangible record will allow a reality check for the child and parents. Consider giving a brief pre-test to allow for a reality check of their mastery before doing poorly on the test.

☐ Two sets of books might be useful. A set of books for home, as well as a set of books to keep at school, will eliminate many stressful trips back to school to pick up textbooks.

☐ Use tangible methods to externalize problem areas:

- ○ Explicitly state out loud the problem and consequences at the time of the event.

- Use timers and planners to break down tasks into manageable, concrete chunks. Timers and planners give a tangible face to the nebulous concept of time, and will also help keep adults from nagging.

- Brainstorm ideas on index cards or word processor. Then, physically sort through and put the topics in order.

☐ Keep it up. Don't allow the success of organizational support to lead to its disuse. Unfortunately, once a program works, the problem seems to no longer exist, and everyone stops helping out. People may confuse the success of the program with the lack of need for it. ("Why should I check Johnny's homework when he hasn't missed any for weeks?") Unfortunately, the same problems will tend to reoccur as soon as the support is withdrawn. It's a disability, remember? The need to keep it up is discussed further in the next chapter.

☐ Provide feedback for any medication treatment. In addition to the above treatments, many children with ADHD benefit from medication. Often, medication will provide the basic neurological skills needed in order to comply with behavioral approaches. When prescribed for people who have ADHD, they stimulate the frontal parts of the brain that are not inhibiting ("filtering out") distractions as well as they should. The medications work similarly to caffeine. The children appear "calmer" because they are more focused, not because they are sedated. More detailed information is given in Chapter 6.

☐ The largest multimodal treatment trial on ADHD showed that most community-based physicians do not provide optimal medication doses (MTA Cooperative Group 1999). Improved feedback from the schools would help identify times and areas where further improvement is still possible. Evaluations need to be done on a child's performance in different subjects at different times of the day. Teachers may use a Connor's Rating Scale or other checklist form, which provide quick feedback. Or, just use a brief written paragraph or two on the child's progress from each teacher. Teacher feedback is essential to the diagnosis and care of children with ADHD.

Encourage use of a word processor

For many students with learning disabilities, ready access to a word processor is essential. There are many enticing computer games for learning to type at home. It is okay if the kids look at their hands while typing. After all, there is no handwritten rough draft that they need to keep their eyes on. Once students have learned basic comfort on the keyboard, then homework and instant messaging will provide the needed practice. The goal is to get the typist up and running quickly.

There is a multitude of advantages for the use of word processors for ADHD students. It helps with dysgraphia, which is a major problem for the vast majority of people with ADHD. The keyboard frees the child's mind to focus on ideas rather than letter formation. In addition, spell-check and grammar-check are lifesavers. Don't worry—the child still has to decide which spelling suggestion to use. Let's just hope we can get them to look at those squiggly red and green lines. Easy ability to make corrections will also encourage the child to accept editing suggestions from the parent/teacher, since that does not mean copying the whole thing over. Further, easy editing may make it simpler for children with writer's block—just start typing something. You can come back later for corrections. Be assured that learning to use a word processor is a basic life skill. There will be very little serious written work in the children's future that does not include one. All they really need to do by hand in the future is sign their name.

For pre-typists, parental use of a word processor lets the child focus on the more important aspects of the assignment. If a child has a writing problem, then consider having the child write or type what he can in the amount of time that the assignment is expected to take, and then let him dictate the rest to the parent. It is better to learn how to tell a creative story than it is to suffer unproductively through dysgraphia.

Elementary school teachers may be uncomfortable with the use of a word processor in class. The bell rings, the child runs out, and now the teacher is left feeling responsible for this expensive machine sitting in the middle of the classroom. In this setting, a good compromise is to allow the child to practice handwriting in class, and typing at home. Students may feel stigmatized by the use of a word processor. This often resolves by secondary school. We can only push the child so far.

If possible, the child's homework station should be equipped with its own basic computer and printer. It is not reasonable to expect a child with homework/ADHD problems to go back and forth between multiple work areas. No games or internet connection should be on the child's machine. They are much too distracting. Be aware that games seem to have their own mysterious habit of loading themselves on to a child's computer.

"Section 504" accommodations

Often, a child needs more than the "common sense" accommodations given above. In the United States, appropriate accommodations can be mandated under two different laws: "Section 504" and IDEA.

Section 504 of the Vocational Rehabilitation Act (Public Law 93–112) is a federal civil rights law that aims at eliminating discrimination in any program that receives federal funds (including most all US schools and colleges). By Section 504 definitions, the disability can be physical or mental; and must substantially limit one or more "life activities" such as learning, performing manual tasks, caring for oneself, speaking, hearing, or walking.

Accommodations like those listed previously under "common sense" can be mandated via Section 504 if needed. Parents or the school may initiate a 504 evaluation. Such classification will usually require a school meeting, but less formal psychological and educational testing than classification under IDEA (see below). Typically, 504 accommodations may be easier to obtain as they generally mandate accommodations more than costly special services. A written plan for 504 accommodations is typically periodically revised (yearly). Extended time on tests, including for the US college entrance SATs, may require classification.

IDEA classification

The US Individuals with Disabilities Education Act (IDEA, Part B) of 1990 provides federal funding to schools that guarantee special needs students with appropriate rights and services, including a free and appropriate public education. If unable to provide an "appropriate" public education, the school must pay for alternate education. IDEA classifiable conditions include:

- specific learning disability (LD)

- emotional and behavioral disorder (ED)

- other health impaired (OHI). The US Dept. of Education memo of 1991 includes ADHD as a classifying condition under OHI.

Parents must be full partners in the process of developing an Individualized Education Plan (IEP). If nothing else, parents certainly know what has not worked so far. IDEA classification evaluations and provided services are usually more comprehensive than 504 plans. The school has the right to decide what evaluation is needed, although the parents may request an independent evaluation if they disagree with the school's evaluation. There is annual updating of the IEP, with full re-evaluation every three years. However, the parents may request review and revision of the IEP at any time. Detailed information can be found through the National Dissemination Center for Children and Youth with Disabilities (see References).

Pop quiz on school and ADHD

The following questions are prompted by this event:

It was open house night for parents of sixth graders who were just entering middle school. The teacher stands up and begins by announcing to the parents, "This is a good year for your children to fail." Needless to say, parents didn't think that this (or any other year) was a good time for that to happen. Jaws dropped.

What the teacher meant, I assume, was that typical children learn from their mistakes (such as not doing their homework), and that this was a safe time for them to learn their lesson—before it shows up on their transcripts for college. In other words, most children learn from a "sink or swim" approach. Sixth grade is a pretty good time to learn the lesson. Unfortunately, most does not apply to children with ADHD.

1. For children with a disability such as blindness, it makes sense to use a "sink or swim" approach to reading the standard textbook.

   (a) True.

   (b) False.

2. For children with a disability such as being disorganized, it makes sense to use a "sink or swim" approach to getting their assignments handed in on time.

   (a) True.

   (b) False.

3. In the US, punishing a child with a recognized organizational disability (essentially all kids with ADHD) is neither useful nor legal.

   (a) True.

   (b) False.

4. Punishment with a grade of zero is appropriate, likely to change the behavior next time, and likely to teach the organizational skills which are lacking.

   (a) True.

   (b) False.

5. It makes sense for a teacher to keep handing out more and more zeros, hoping that will finally overcome the disability.

   (a) True.

   (b) False.

6. A better approach would be to make sure the work is handed in (see this chapter), or at worst, to give a grade of 65.

   (a) True.

   (b) False.

7. Teachers can't make such accommodations for everyone, but they can for children with recognized ADHD.

   (a) True.

   (b) False.

Answers:

1. (b), 2. (b), 3. (a), 4. (b), 5. (b), 6. (a), 7. (a).

Chapter 5

Rule #4: Keep It Going

Rule #4 is simple to state but hard to accomplish: keep it going. In other words, keep doing Rules #1–3. ADHDers are born with a neurologically different brain (see the biological findings in Chapter 1). The issues are not going away overnight. Neither will the need for support.

They already know what to do. They just can't do it

It's not that kids with ADHD don't know what to do. If you gave them a quiz on correct behavior, they'd already get 100% right. For example, do you think your children can correctly answer the following questions?

- Should you write down all of your assignments?

- Should you plan ahead for all of your projects?

- Should you yell at your mother when she is trying to help you?

- Should you come to dinner when you are called?

- Should you stop "overreacting?"

- Should you stop "shooting yourself in the foot?"

See! They'd get a score of 100% on correct behavior. You've taught them all they need to know! Phew! You're done! Done, except for one (big) problem: although they know what to do, they just cannot carry out the plan. That's because their disability is exactly in the area of making a plan happen. The caregivers will need to keep up their "scaffolding" of support in the area of executing a plan (Brown 2005). The teachers and parents will need to avoid falling prey to the "garage mechanic approach" (Smith *et al.* 2006, p.83) of ADHD intervention: the idea that we can drop these kids off somewhere like a psychologist or resource room for a few months, and that they will then be "fixed" and able to fly on their own. Unfortunately, that doesn't work any better than telling a blind child "You shouldn't need books in Braille, anymore." So, you, or some other surrogate frontal lobe provider, will likely need to be there for some time to come. Teachers and parents are going to have to keep "getting their hands dirty" (Smith *et al.* 2006, p.82). Sorry.

Keep providing help for deficits at the moment it is needed

Since this neurologically-based problem is not going away this week, we have two choices: keep providing help for the deficits of ADHD before the kids make mistakes, or keep punishing the child after he makes the mistakes.

Once we understand that negative reinforcement after the fact has not been working (it hasn't yet, has it?), we are ready to provide relief for their disabilities by guiding ADHDers at the moment guidance is needed—rather than continued disbelief that they did it wrong again. We may be amazed at how many times the kids keep using the same unsuccessful strategies, but how many times is it going to take for us to figure out that we keep using unsuccessful strategies with them. And when the interventions are working, don't confuse the success of those interventions with a lack of need for them.

Provide a safety net

When acrobats are taught a new trapeze act, their trainers provide them with a safety net. When gymnasts perform their high bar routines, they have a "spotter." No one worries that providing these safeguards will interfere with learning, or make the performer take his task less seriously. It is simply that without a safety net, the penalty for missing a handgrip while flying across the trapeze bars is neither commensurate with the

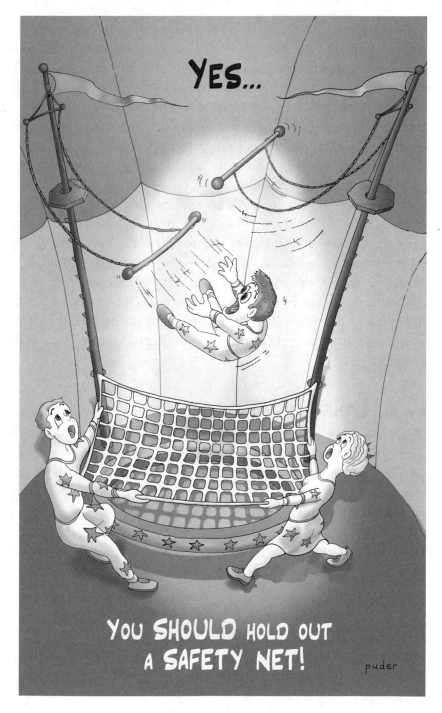

Figure 9: Be the child's safety net

mistake nor productive. Similarly, we may need to intervene in the child's college application process, because the penalty of messing up his future career is not commensurate with the "sin" of poor organization when it comes to filling out forms (see Figure 9).

Be the safety net or "spotter" for the special needs kid. If she gets it right on her own, she won't need you, and there's no harm done that you were standing by. If she doesn't get it right, then you were there to provide a softer landing—and make sure that the consequence was appropriate to the mistake.

Note the big difference between being a "crutch" (which is a bad idea) and being a "safety net" (which is a good idea). Being a crutch would mean helping with each and every step for the child, never letting him even try to learn to walk on his own. Being a safety net, though, is standing actively in the background while the child does most of the work on his own—but you are there for the more rare occasion when he actually is about to falter. If he doesn't end up needing you, there's no harm that you were there. If he does need you, then you can provide a safe landing.

Be patient. This is the 50-year plan

As flight controller Gene Kranz said on the Apollo 13 mission, "Failure is not an option." If it is not working, try something else. However, don't expect that all problems can be fixed overnight. Many of these kids will be working on their issues as part of a "50-year plan." In the meantime, remember that threats may change behavior, but they do not produce a good attitude. Only success and rewards (internal or external) can do that. This is not war. We are all on the same team. Keep it up, and give it time. It is hard work, but you will make it through this. You have no other choice.

Chapter 6

Medication Treatments for ADHD

This information does not constitute medical advice. Available information is often quite limited. Recommendations need to be taken as subject to change and debate. Medications in children are used frequently in age groups and for indications that are not US FDA approved. This information is not intended to be all-inclusive. Full discussion of the usefulness, indications, side effects, risks, monitoring, drug interactions, etc., of these medications is beyond this book. Check with your doctor, the package insert, and www.FDA.gov for new and complete information. Medical treatment of the associated disorders is perhaps best done in consultation with a neurologist or psychiatrist.

Thoughts on medicating little children

It sounds pretty horrible…medicating children to control their behavior. What is society coming to? Before getting down to specifics, we need to address some very legitimate concerns.

Who are we giving psychotropic medications to?

If you were lucky enough to have received a "neurotypical," well-functioning brain—great for you! You were very fortunate, indeed. If you were lucky enough to have received a somewhat atypically functioning brain that does, however, respond to environmental manipulations—good for you, too. But if you were handed an atypical brain for which accommodations, bribes, and threats didn't solve the problem—your brain may indeed need a helping hand from medication. It's not that you chose to be that way. It's the biological hand you were dealt.

Practically speaking, medication is never our first or only choice of treatment. By the time a child is brought to my office, years' worth of attempts to finesse, cajole, and punish have already been tried. Too much pain has been already endured, and way too many tears have been already shed. True, lots of behavioral strategies can help tremendously. Indeed, the entire rest of this book is dedicated to them. If they work well enough, keep doing them. If not, try adding something else. For many children, that something else to try is medication. You are making that decision because you love the child, and nothing else is helping.

The largest, national US study on ADHD treatments, called the MTA (1999) study, clearly showed that medication—especially tightly, professionally supervised use of medication—was clearly the most effective treatment strategy. Medication was far more beneficial than even the best and most aggressive patient and family counseling strategies.

We need to stop blaming people for having a psychiatric condition

In order to understand why behavioral approaches may be insufficient in ADHD, we need to apply modern, scientific understanding to the condition. As we saw in Chapter 1, ADHD is typically a biological problem. The chances of having ADHD are 90% in your genes. It's not usually bad parenting. (After all, look how your other children turned out.) It's not lack of will power on the part of your child. It's brain chemistry, just like epilepsy and migraines. We don't tell a person with epilepsy to "Just get your act together!" We don't tell a person screaming in pain from a migraine that she just needs more willpower in order to stop her vomiting and headache. It currently makes perfect sense to use anticonvulsants for seizures, just like it makes sense to use insulin for diabetes when diet does not work. Unfortunately, many of us are still a few centuries behind when it comes to psychiatric disease, blaming it on the very people who are trying to cope with their conditions. When behavioral and environmental interventions do not work, then it makes sense to use biochemical interventions, i.e., medications, for biochemical problems.

How will people ever learn to handle their own problems if they rely on medication?

Once again, medications are to be added after behavioral attempts to get the child to handle his problem(s) have already failed, or to make those interventions more likely to succeed. Without medication to address their neurobiological differences, some people just don't have the basic brain hardware with which to comply. Once you have given a child a reasonable attention span with medication, then we can ask him to behave in class. Importantly, we are not saying to use medication instead of teaching coping skills; we are saying that sometimes medication is needed to make utilizing those techniques actually possible.

Don't worry about medication being used as a quick fix, causing us to be too soft on these kids. They are already having a tough life, and even on medication, their life will still be tougher than typical. The medications are not perfect, and there will still be plenty of opportunity to build character. The innate problems will continue, but it will now be a doable and a more fair fight.

Are they going to need medication for the rest of their lives?

They will need medication for as long as they need it. In the past, the disappearance of physical hyperactivity by the teenage years led many people to believe that ADHD resolved during adolescence. However, we now understand that although the hyperactivity usually abates (have you ever seen a 60-year-old man jump out of a shopping cart?), the inattention and executive function problems persist into adulthood in half of the kids. For most, that will mean that medication will be needed at least through high school or college. After that, many people can get themselves into lifestyles that better fit their strengths and interests. The fortunate ones also learn to gracefully accept support from surrogate frontal lobes donated by spouses, secretaries, partners, lawyers, and accountants.

Additional frontal lobe growth during young adulthood will hopefully lead to even further progress.

How do ADHD medications work?

Stimulants work by increasing the levels of two brain transmitters: dopamine and norepinephrine. These neurotransmitters wake up the frontal and pre-frontal lobe braking functions, allowing them to exert better executive function in areas such as distractibility and self-control. Stimulant medications provide self-control by waking up (stimulating) the brain's own brakes.

Most people assume that if a kid is running all around the classroom, and you slip him a pill, after which he then sits down quietly, then the pill must have somehow made him too tired to get up and bother anyone. Nothing could be further from the truth. If we use an automobile analogy for ADHD, we see that ADHDers are like cars without brakes. They careen around, unable to stop (inhibit) their actions. Now, sedatives would be analogous to pouring tar on the car's gears—making the child too tired to bother anyone or get into trouble. That would be a horrible thing to do. However, stimulants are *not* like sedatives. Stimulants work by fixing (stimulating) the car's brakes. They make a higher performing machine (see Figure 10).

This is such an important point that we'll use another analogy—the coffee break. The boss comes into the room at 10:30 am and finds a group of well-intentioned but tired secretaries chatting about what they had for dinner last night. Nothing useful is getting done. Fortunately, the coffee break is finally here. People get up to stretch and more blood flows to their brain. Caffeine from the coffee wakes up (stimulates) the frontal lobes. The boss comes back after the coffee break and now finds a quiet room—just the continuous clicking of keyboards. So what happened during coffee break? Did the coffee make the secretaries no longer surprisingly interested in finding out what the others had for dinner last night? Did the coffee make them too tired to chat? No, just the opposite. The caffeine woke up their frontal lobes. The secretaries are quiet after coffee because they are awake and functioning productively, just like they always wanted to, but couldn't when they were tired.

Figure 10: Stimulant medications provide self-control by waking up (stimulating) the brain's brakes

There is nothing paradoxical about stimulants having a "calming" effect in children versus adults. In any age person (child, teen, or adult), they continue to function in the same fashion—they wake up the person's brakes. The person sits still because he is now properly awake and capable of self-control, not because he is sedated. It's like overtired children who behave more calmly after a good night's sleep refreshes their frontal lobes.

What are the benefits of medication?

So, what do we hope will happen when we give stimulant medication to a child? We expect to see a significant improvement in attention span, and a significant reduction in hyperactivity and impulsivity. The teachers should notice resolution of previous problems with incomplete class work, distractibility, and disruptive behavior. Parents should notice that homework goes much more efficiently, and family outings go more smoothly with fewer outbursts (on the part of both the parents and child).

The child often notices nothing. Indeed, towards the beginning of each follow-up visit, I usually ask the child, "Do you notice anything when you take the medication?" The usual response of a younger boy is, "Huh?" We next ask, "Is there anything that you don't like about the medication? We might get an answer such as, "I don't like the way the capsule tastes," or "Well, I'm not very hungry at lunch, but I eat a huge dinner." Next, we move to the questions, "Can you pay attention better? Are you doing better in school? Are you getting along better with your parents?" The answers are usually, "Yes." This is what I want to hear. I don't want the child to feel any different on the medication. After all, how can you become addicted to a non-feeling? When asked to think about it, though, children can usually appreciate that their life is going better, and that life doesn't seem to go as well when they don't take it. It's reassuring that the medication typically does not take the "twinkle" out of the kid's eyes, just like secretaries who drink coffee still have the twinkle in their eyes. They have the same energy. Now, however, they can focus that energy on one activity until it is done, before moving to the next.

Handwriting also seems to improve markedly for many kids. Improvement in organization may not be as robust as in the other areas, and will likely still need support.

What are the side effects of stimulant medications?

I wish that your child had no problems. And I wish that doctors had medications that had zero side effects. Really, I do. It's just that our wishes have not been granted yet. No one can promise you that there are no side effects to the medications. (There are.) No one can promise you that we won't discover in the next half-century some side effects that we haven't discovered in the first half-century of their use. But we have to make a decision now, based upon what we know now about the risks and benefits both of taking medication and of not taking medication.

The risks of not being on medication

Remember, there are huge known risks to ADHD that isn't properly brought under control. These include, among many others:

- a 30% risk of substance abuse

- high risk of dropping out of high school or college

- poor self-esteem

- high risk of car accidents.

The risks of being on medication

Possible side effects include:

- Insomnia (trouble falling asleep). This is somewhat frequent, but usually improves over time.

- Loss of appetite, especially for lunch. This is also somewhat frequent, but again usually improves over time.

- A few pounds weight loss, which then typically stabilizes as the child subsequently gains weight as expected.

- Concerns over height, i.e., that some children might be a fraction shorter than they might have been otherwise. For the overwhelming number of children, stimulants do not "stunt your growth."

- Tics. Stimulants clearly can exacerbate tics in some children who are prone to them. Most authorities would agree that in the vast majority of times, the tics would improve (to where they would have been anyway) when the medication dose is lowered or withdrawn. At times, the tic exacerbation may not improve when the medication is withdrawn. In these unlikely cases, it is not clear that this is not just a chance association in time.

- Anxiety/OCD symptoms. These may become exacerbated by stimulants.

- Changes in personality, including irritability and negative behaviors. In particular, patients prone to mania or bipolar disorder may have a significant negative reaction, including the induction of a manic spell.

- Headaches.

- Stomachaches (which are minimized by taking the medication after a meal).

- Concerns over cardiac issues. The US FDA has labeled all first-line ADHD medications as possessing a possible small risk for being associated with sudden death—especially if the patient has issues such as structural heart disease, fainting, certain kinds of arrhythmias (irregular heart beats); or a family history such as certain kinds of heart problems, arrhythmias, or sudden unexplained death. These issues should be discussed with your physician, and may lead to a cardiac evaluation.

- Very small increases in heart rate and blood pressure.

Please talk to your doctor.

What about "rebound" irritability?

"Rebound" occurs in some people when the medication level is wearing down quickly. Suddenly, the child becomes unusually nasty, tearful, and irrational. For example, all of the sudden, the child wants a certain kind of cookie. It doesn't matter that there is no such cookie in the house. It doesn't matter that the store stopped selling them years ago. It doesn't matter that there are even better cookies in the cupboard. It's Mom's fault, and it's the end of the world. There's no reasoning. Just yelling. A half hour later, he's back to normal. You can tell that it is "rebound" (not direct medication effect) by the timing of the irritability. If it were a direct effect of the medication, it would be occurring an hour or two after taking the medication, as the medication level is peaking. If it's rebound, the reaction occurs many hours later, as the medication is wearing off. Note that the term "rebound" does not refer to the majority of times when the medication merely wears off and the child returns to his typical baseline, unmedicated state.

There are several ways to handle rebound. The long-lasting preparations seem to engender less rebound than the short-acting ones. Or, a tiny "touch-up" dose of a short-acting preparation can be given about 30 to 60 minutes before the rebound starts. This slows the sudden drop in medication level that was causing the symptoms. Or, now that you know what's going on, you can all just stay out of each other's way until the rebound is over. Be sure that the rebound-like behavior is not simply late afternoon hunger due to poor lunchtime appetite.

Are stimulants addicting?

Multiple studies (see review by Wilens *et al.* 2003) show that the use of stimulants in ADHD children is associated with a greatly reduced risk of future substance abuse (when compared to ADHD children who are not successfully treated). Presumably, those kids whose life is filled with success do not need to turn to alternate forms of seeking pleasure.

The different "stimulant" medications

Stimulants are medications that raise dopamine as well as norepinephrine levels. The stimulants currently used for the treatment of ADHD are based primarily on two sets of chemicals: methylphenidate-based medications, and amphetamine-based medications. Each is available in short- and long-acting formulations.

Methylphenidate preparations (short-acting)

□ *Ritalin (methylphenidate)*. Ritalin is a brand name for the generic chemical called methylphenidate. Methylphenidate has been the gold standard of stimulant treatment for ADHD. Regular Ritalin requires frequent dosing since the tablets last only three to four hours. This created the need for the stigmatizing and inconvenient lunchtime trip to the school nurse. Even the lunch dose of Ritalin wore off by the end of school. Well-intentioned mothers would try to avoid giving an afternoon dose, leading to increased arguments at homework time.

□ *Focalin (d-methylphenidate)*. Focalin is just the active part of methyl-phenidate (just the d-isomer). It requires only half of the dose of the regular methylphenidate compound, and seems to last a little longer—up to four or five hours.

Methylphenidate preparations (long-acting)

The traditional short-acting forms of methylphenidate are being largely replaced by long-lasting ones. Although they contain the exact same chemical as regular Ritalin, these formulations use varying technologies to keep releasing the medication throughout the day. Long-lasting prepa-rations avoid the need for the lunchtime dose from the nurse, have less rebound, and some last through homework time. They are typically taken once a day, at breakfast time.

□ *Concerta*. Concerta, the first good long-acting preparation of methylphenidate to be marketed, approximates the release of three doses of methylphenidate. It has an effective life of about 10+ hours. Concerta is designed to release relatively less during the morning, and a higher proportion of medication later in the day. Although there may be good research reasons for designing it that way, some children on Concerta benefit from an additional morning boost from a short-acting preparation. The pills are fairly small, but must be swallowed intact.

□ *Metadate CD*. "CD" stands for "controlled delivery." This capsule uses beads that release their methylphenidate at two different times, to approximate a twice a day dosage. The formulation releases somewhat more of its medication in the morning than does Concerta.

It works during school for eight hours. For children unable to swallow the intact capsule, it can be opened and sprinkled on a low fat food such as apple sauce, followed by a drink of water. Beaded preparations should not be chewed.

☐ *Ritalin LA.* "LA" stands for "long-acting." This capsule also uses beads, but is designed to replicate two equal doses at a four-hour interval. It thus creates a useful life limited to the school hours. Ritalin LA capsules can also be opened and sprinkled on apple sauce, followed by a drink of water.

☐ *Daytrana.* This is a methylphenidate skin patch, which is applied daily to the child's hip area. Since the patch can be removed at any time, it may be helpful for children who require different lengths of treatment duration on different days. Children may develop skin irritation or even allergic reactions to the methylphenidate or other patch components.

Amphetamine-based preparations

☐ *Dexedrine* is the brand name for dextro-amphetamine. Dexedrine comes in tablets with a four-hour effect; and as Dexedrine Spansules, which have a ten-hour effect. These excellent preparations seem to have been replaced by a mixed amphetamine salt preparation marketed under the brand name Adderall. Note that amphetamines used orally as prescribed do not have the "highs" or crashes associated with the very different usage by drug abusers.

☐ *Adderall* is the brand name for a combination of mixed amphetamine salts. There is a tablet form that has a four- to six-hour effect. There is also a long-lasting capsule form that has a 10+ hour effect called *Adderall XR* ("XR" stands for "eXtended Release"). The capsules can be swallowed whole, or sprinkled on apple sauce. There is currently a generic form of Adderall tablets in the US, but not for the Adderall XR capsules.

Cylert (pemoline)

☐   *Cylert* (the brand name for pemoline) is rarely started any more due to possible rare liver toxicity.

Which stimulant to use?

Most doctors do not feel that there is compelling evidence to use one stimulant over the other. If one class of stimulants does not work, or causes certain side effects, then trial with another preparation should be considered. In general, the long-lasting preparations make more sense than the shorter-acting ones. Younger children may only require one of the eight-hour preparations; whereas, once homework sets in, an even longer-acting formulation would make more sense. Regardless, sometimes an afternoon dose of a short-acting preparation needs to be added to get through the rest of the day. If a dose is missed, just pick up with the regular dose at the next scheduled time. Do not double up the next dose.

How will the doctor monitor this medicine?

The doctor may ask for regular reports from your child's teacher(s) to check on learning and behavior. The medical staff will follow height, weight, pulse, and blood pressure. When Cylert is used, blood is taken to check on the liver function and blood count—usually before starting the medicine, and periodically afterward.

What about weekends and vacations?

In the beginning trial period, I ask the parents to give the stimulant medications seven days a week. This way, they can see for themselves how the child acts on medication. That knowledge is useful to the doctor and is good for the parents' peace of mind. In addition, the only way to know whether the medication will help in the home setting is to try it there! Once we have this knowledge in place, the parents can choose whether or not to use stimulant medication during non-school hours by answering a simple question: "If my child took the medication now, would he have a more positive experience over the next few hours?" For example, would homework go more smoothly? Would a trip to the mall be a more positive experience for everyone? Would the ballgame or birthday party go better? Would Dad take him to the hardware store all alone? Isn't your child's relationship with you, the rest of her family, and her friends as important as her school grades? If the medication is causing unwanted side effects, such as significant appetite suppression, then we may need to be more restrictive in its non-school usage. Medically, it is usually safe to start and stop stimulant medication as needed for weekends and brief vacations.

Medications below such as Strattera, alpha-2 agonists, and antidepressants need to be taken regularly seven days a week, and need to be started and tapered off slowly.

Other medications for ADHD

In addition to the stimulant medications above, there are several other medicines that may also be useful for the treatment of ADHD.

Strattera (atomoxetine)

The US FDA (Food and Drug Administration) approved Strattera in 2002 for the treatment of ADHD. It directly increases just norepinephrine levels in multiple brain areas, although it indirectly increases dopamine levels in the frontal lobes. As such, it is more "selective" than the stimulants. Data suggest that it does not typically increase tics, insomnia, or anxiety in ADHD patients; and that it may have a role in improving family interactions over a 24-hour period. Strattera may take four to six weeks to show its degree of effectiveness. More direct comparisons with the stimulants and more long-term follow up will be needed.

The most common side effects with Strattera have been sedation and diminished appetite. Insomnia, headaches, and weight loss are also fairly common. Ramping up the dose very slowly over several weeks can help to diminish the incidence of these side effects. There also have been rare cases of liver inflammation with Strattera. Let your doctor know immediately if your child experiences jaundice (yellow eyes or skin), pain in the upper right part of the abdomen (where the liver is), very dark urine, very itchy skin, or "unexplained flu-like symptoms." Strattera might also possibly rarely increase the risk of agitated or manic behaviors. In addition, there have been warnings about Strattera and possible increased thoughts of self-harm. This has led to a US FDA call for close monitoring of the medication, especially when starting (or changing) the dosage—which typically should be done slowly. The FDA has also recently posted cardiac warnings for Strattera that are similar to those for the stimulants (see above).

Catapres (clonidine) and guanfacine (Tenex)

Catapres (clonidine) and Tenex (guanfacine) are "alpha-2 agonists," which have been used chiefly as anti-hypertensive medications in adults. They have been of some use in children with attention deficit problems, particularly for the symptom of impulsivity. They are also used in the treatment of children with tic disorders, such as in Tourette's syndrome. These medications have a potential sedating effect and are probably best given at bedtime initially. Catapres is sometimes used in kids who have insomnia to allow them to go to sleep at night at a more reasonable hour. Headaches, dizziness, and fatigue are occasional problems with the use of these medications, and need to be monitored carefully. Blood pressure needs to be periodically followed, but rarely becomes a significant problem. Sudden changes in the regimen (such as suddenly stopping the medication) can cause dangerous blood pressure swings, and should be avoided. These medications need to be taken seven days a week. Care must be exercised with use of alpha-2 agonists in combination with stimulants. Discuss this with your doctor.

Tofranil (imipramine)

This "tricyclic antidepressant" is sometimes used in the treatment of ADHD. It provides some improvement of inattention, and has an anti-anxiety effect, as well. There may be an improved ability to tolerate frustration, and the child may appear to be more outgoing and sociable as well. When given before bedtime, it may also allow the child to fall asleep more readily.

Tofranil has been used for many years by pediatricians in the treatment of bedwetting. In this regard, it has a long safety record. All medicines, of course, have side effects, and Tofranil has its own special list.

Perhaps the greatest concern is the small possibility of a potential adverse effect on the heart. An EKG may be monitored. Additionally, there are very rare case reports of liver and bone marrow toxicity. If a child is maintained on such medication for any length of time, routine blood work to check these functions and drug levels may be performed. Occasionally, fatigue, constipation, dry mouth, blurry vision, and rapid heartbeat may occur. Unlike stimulant medication, Tofranil does not work immediately, but often takes several weeks before there is any perceived benefit.

Tofranil, like other tricyclic medications, is used as an antidepressant in adults (but does not seem to be effective for depression in children). Even when not taking antidepressant medications for depression, children and young adults should be monitored for possible increased thoughts of self-harm.

Wellbutrin (bupropion)

Wellbutrin is considered a "novel antidepressant" with dopamine and noradrenergic effects. It may improve aggression and hyperactivity, as well as cognition and inattention. It may be helpful for depression and anxiety, but has no effect on obsessive/compulsive behavior. Although usually well tolerated, it may rarely precipitate tics, seizures, mania, depression, weight loss, and headaches. Patients with eating disorders or a history of seizures are at special risk. Again, especially children and young adults on antidepressants should be watched for thoughts of self-harm. As with all medication use, ask your doctor for full details.

Medication for co-occurring disorders

Medication treatment for the co-occurring disorders associated with ADHD are discussed in Chapter 1.

Chapter 7

For Kids to Read

What happened to my brakes?

Imagine this: A kid is on a bicycle speeding downhill. The world is whizzing by. He needs to avoid holes in the pavement. The road is curving. The wind buzzes in his ear, and makes his eyes tear.

Suddenly, there are rocks in the road! He goes to put on the brakes—but they don't work!! As the bike speeds downhill, just staying on it seems overwhelming. So much is going on! So much seems out of control. Who has time to pay attention to the huge truck coming?

That's the life of someone with Attention Deficit Hyperactivity Disorder (ADHD). It all comes from difficulty "putting on the brakes," to borrow the title of a wonderful book by Patricia Quinn and Judith Stern (2001).

Here's what's happening. Your brain's "boss" is located in your "frontal lobes," which are located in the front part of your brain. (Touch your forehead. Just behind that is where the frontal lobe boss lives.) These frontal lobes figure out where you want to go, and the step-by-step plan of how to get there. Like any boss, a large part of their job is saying, "No!" For example, your parents are supposed to be the boss in your house. Think how often their job is to say, "No!" They're always saying things like, "Susan, do not have a fifth scoop of ice-cream," or, "Bob, stop playing Nintendo so that you can do your homework," or, "Jill, don't stay out past 10 pm." Unless something puts brakes on our actions, we would spin out of control. Our frontal lobes are our own brakes.

Well, at least that is how it is supposed to work. In ADHD kids, the front part of their brains—the boss—doesn't do a good job of putting on the brakes. It's like the boss is asleep on the job. This means that these kids may:

* Have trouble putting brakes on distractions. Their minds are pulled off the main topic by anything more "interesting." They may even find playing with a paperclip more "interesting" than doing their homework. They are like moths—always attracted to the brightest light—even if that is not where they are supposed to be. This leads to the "Attention Deficit" of ADHD. (See Figure 3, p.24.)

* Have trouble sitting still rather than checking out those distractions. This leads to the "Hyperactivity" of ADHD.

* Have trouble putting brakes on any thought that floats into their minds. This includes trouble putting brakes on frustrations and overreactions. This leads to "impulsivity," which is acting before you think.

No wonder things go out of control so often!

Why don't I see problems coming?

Let's imagine another scene: Jack is in a boat, happily fishing. Reeling in the jiggling fish while still steering the boat captures all of his attention. (See Figure 4, p.26 and Figure 5, p.27.) Jack is so busy catching the fish that he can't look ahead to see the waterfall coming up! It's not that he doesn't care about the cliff! After all, he doesn't want to fall off a cliff any more than anyone else does. It's just that he never gets the chance to see what's coming up. Just like the speeding bicyclist, the future comes as a surprise to ADHD kids. This is called a lack of "foresight." So, a person with ADHD:

* may not think about what will be best even for himself. Other people might think wrongly that he doesn't care.

* may not think about what will be best for other people. Other people might think wrongly that he is selfish or mean.

What other problems are common for ADHD kids?

Teachers, parents, and friends may notice other problems for kids who have ADHD. These kids might also:

* be very disorganized. They often don't get the right assignments home. Even more amazing, they may do homework and then can't find it or forget to hand it in!

* seem "spacey"

* find that other people seem to take forever to eat, shop, or get to the point!

* argue, blame others, or even lie

* sometimes have "blow ups" over unimportant things

* yell at people who are trying to help them

* have trouble noticing how other people are reacting to them. After all, who's got time for that?

* often feel nervous or worried

* have trouble with handwriting, or sometimes with other school subjects.

What can we do about it?

Hundreds of books have been written about helping kids with ADHD. Here's some of the best advice:

☼ Just STOP. Remember, the problem in ADHD is trouble putting on the brakes. Warning signs that our brakes aren't working include getting angry, raising our voice, and tightening our hands. If you are yelling, then you may be about to spin out of control! STOP! Tell your parents (or teachers), "I need five minutes of chill-out time." Go someplace quiet, such as your room. Do something calm, like reading a book, sorting cards, or playing with Legos. (Activities such as Nintendo or television do not make good chill-out activities—no one will be able to get you away from them!) Your parents should also take advantage of "chill-out time." Once everyone is calm, then come back for a useful discussion of the problem (see Figure 8, p.72).

☼ Make decisions when you are calm. You'll be surprised how much easier it is to reach a good decision when you and your parents are calm. People cannot think clearly when they are overexcited. Returning to our bicycle example, wait until the bicycle coasts to a stop. Then, look around and calmly consider your options. Once calm, everyone gets to make his or her points heard, and work out a solution that everyone can accept (see Figure 7, p.71).

☼ Even better, solve the problems before they come up. For example, if your parents are always frustrating you when they call you to come down to dinner, talk to them about it! Let them know how much it frustrates you. Also, ask them what their needs are. Then, solve the problem. For example, maybe your parents could give you five-minute and two-minute warnings, and even then allow an extra minute to come to dinner. (But keep it to just one extra minute.) This is called "problem solving." Chapter 3 contains details for you and your parents to work on this technique.

☼ Realize that your parents and teachers are usually good at preparing for the future. In the bicycle story above, your parents can be thought of as standing on the sidewalk, watching you speed downhill. Since they are not over-whelmed by the bike ride, they have no trouble looking ahead to see the truck coming. They're screaming, "Watch out for the truck!" or, "Watch out for that cliff," or, "Watch out for that book report due in two weeks." A parent's fore-sight is typically much better than that of their ADHD child. Listen to them. Please. If nothing else, it's probably fair to say that your parents usually try to act in your best interest—even if they do make the wrong choices every once in a while!

☼ Kids with ADHD typically need help with organization. Take it. When you get older, you can hire a secretary to help you. But right now, you probably can't afford your own secretary. Do you know anyone at home that you can trust, and who is willing to help you for free? (Hint: they're called P-A-R-E-N-T-S.) Teachers at school may be willing to help with organizational skills, also. Remember, it is not fair to yell at someone who is trying to help you!

☼ Use assignment pads, monthly calendars, homework folders and timers to help with organization. These are described in Chapter 4 on "Keep it organized."

☼ Your doctor may prescribe medication with "stimulants" (such as Ritalin, Concerta, Focalin, Adderall or Dexedrine). Like coffee, these medications wake up your frontal lobes, making them perform better. Let's return to the bicycle story. Medications like Ritalin work by strengthening the stopping power of your brakes. You find yourself in less trouble because you now have a high performance bike, which is complete with a braking system. They do not work by making you too tired to move around (see Figure 10, p.111).

☼ Read more about ADHD.

◈ Younger children can read *Putting on the Brakes: Young People's Guide to Understanding Attention Deficit Hyperactivity Disorder* by Patricia Quinn and Judith Stern (2001).

◈ Teenagers can read *Adolescents and ADD: Gaining the Advantage* by Patricia Quinn (1995).

- ◈ High school and college students can read *ADD and the College Student* by Patricia Quinn (2001).

- ◈ Social skills—such as how to make conversations and keep friends—can be improved with the very funny book *How Rude: The Teenager's Guide to Good Manners, Proper Behavior, and Not Grossing People Out* by Alex J. Packer (1997).

☼ Keep a good attitude about yourself. Remember that ADHD kids also have many great traits. They know how to have fun and enjoy the present moment. They are often quite smart, very creative, and have a "Why not try it?" attitude that is the envy of many people. We always need to keep in mind all of those things that are wonderful about you. Get "a kick" out of yourself and other people around you!! (See Figure 11, p.166).

Good luck!

Chapter 8

Summary

We've been missing the point

> Johnny is very active! He never stops moving. He gets distracted by any little noise, and has the attention span of a flea. Often, he acts before he thinks. His sister, Jill, is often in a fog. We're always calling out, "Earth to Jill!"

That is how we typically consider children with attention deficit hyperactivity disorder (ADHD). OK, not so bad. But that is often only the tip of the iceberg. Here is another likely description of the whole picture for an ADHD child:

> I can't take it any more!! We scream all morning to get out of the house. Homework takes hours. If I don't help him with his work, he's so disorganized that he'll never do well. If I do help him, he screams at me. Since he never finishes anything, everyone thinks he doesn't care. No matter how much we beg or punish, he keeps doing the same stupid things over and over again. He never considers the consequences of his actions, and doesn't seem to care if they hurt me. It's so easy for him to get overwhelmed. He is so inflexible and easily frustrated that he blows up over anything. It gets me so angry that I scream back, which makes everything even worse. Now that he's getting older, the lies and the cursing are getting worse, too. I know he has trouble paying attention, but why does he have all of these other problems as well?

It is not a coincidence that children with ADHD often manifest so much more than the classic triad of inattention, impulsivity, and hyperactivity.

When we focus merely on these typically defined symptoms, we barely scratch the surface of the whole range of difficult problems experienced by patients and their families. This spectrum includes a wide range of "executive dysfunction" (such as poor self-control and foresight), additional co-occurring disorders (such as anxiety, depression, or conduct disorders), and family stresses. These are summarized graphically in Figure 2, p.17.

Redefining ADHD to include "executive dysfunction"

ADHD needs to be redefined to include a wide range of "executive dysfunction." As Russell Barkley (2000) explains, this dysfunction stems from an inability to inhibit current behavior so that demands for the future can be met.

So, what are executive functions?

When you step on a snake, it bites. No verbal discussion occurs within the snake's brain. No recall of whether striking back worked in the past. No thought as to where this action will lead in the future. No inhibition. Rather, stepped on; bite back. Humans, fortunately, have the option to modulate their behavior.

No single part of the human brain is solely in charge of this modulation. It does appear, however, that our frontal and pre-frontal lobes function largely as our "chief executive officer (CEO)." Orchestrating language and memory functions from other parts of the brain, these frontal centers consider where we came from, where we want to go, and how to flexibly control ourselves in order to actually get there.

Most importantly, the ability to inhibit (applying our brakes) is central to effective executive function. Successful execution of a plan largely involves putting brakes on distracting activities. These brakes—courtesy of our pre-frontal inhibitory centers—allow us the luxury of time during which we can consider our options before reacting.

This lack of inhibition is a double problem for people with ADHD. First, without these brakes, they will be viewed as unable to adequately inhibit distractions, inhibit impulsive reactions, or inhibit physically acting upon these stimuli (hyperactivity). Second, patients with ADHD do not inhibit their behavior long enough for the other executive functions below to adequately develop, either. Executive functions identified by Barkley (2000), Brown (2005), and others include:

☐ Initiation is the skill of actually getting started. At some point, you have to stop taking trips to the bathroom and actually start your homework. Procrastination comes naturally. Actually getting down to work (not just intending to!) takes the ability to inhibit all of the other possible activities.

☐ Self-talk refers to the ability to talk to ourselves—a mechanism by which we work through our choices using words. Toddlers can be heard using self-talk out loud. Eventually, this ability becomes internalized and automatic. However, ADHD patients have not inhibited their reactions long enough for this skill to fully develop.

☐ Foresight—keeping the future in mind—will be poor when we are unable to inhibit the current distractions. People with ADHD are prisoners of the present; the future catches them off guard. In fact, surprisingly poor foresight is perhaps the greatest difficulty in their lives, and explains why people with ADHD keep "shooting themselves in their own feet."

☐ Hindsight—keeping the past in mind—is necessary if we are to gain wisdom from our previous experiences in life. A lack of hindsight is one of the reasons that ADHD people tend not to learn from their mistakes.

☐ Working memory refers to those ideas that we can keep active in our minds at a given moment. We have to be able to juggle not just the present situation, but also keep in mind past times when certain strategies did or did not work (hindsight). Working memory hopefully also includes the foresight to keep future goals in mind (such as remembering that we want to get into a good college, not just do the most intriguing activity currently available). Without the ability to inhibit, people with ADHD never get to develop good working memory function.

❑ Sense of time is an executive function that is usually extremely poor in ADHD. The time estimates of ADHDers are notoriously poor—both too short and too long.

❑ Organization is a skill. Some people are good at it. ADHD people are not, almost by definition. As seen in Box 2, p.136, five out of the nine possible criteria of the inattentive category of ADHD are purely organizational—and you only need to meet six of the criteria to qualify for the diagnosis of ADHD.

❑ Flexibility is the skill to alter plans as the circumstances change. The world is an unpredictable place, and plans rarely proceed just as we had imagined. Stuff happens along the way. We need flexibility to readjust our actions in mid-course.

❑ Shifting from Agenda A to Agenda B (transitioning), especially at the time frame of someone else, is a difficult task requiring good executive function. Pulling yourself out of one activity and switching to another is innately difficult, and requires brakes and self-control.

❑ Separating emotion from fact requires time to reflect. Each event in our lives has an objective reality, and an additional "emotional tag" which we attach to it. For example, we return to our car and find a parking ticket on the windshield. Our emotional reaction might be rage over getting a ticket, but the objective fact is that the ticket was only for $5 anyway. Without the gift of time, we never get to separate our huge emotional feeling from what is really a tiny problem. The result is a poor ability to judge the true significance of what is happening to us.

❑ Adding emotion to fact is an important part of "motivation." After all, it's hard to be motivated if you have no gut emotions about the activity. So, typical working memory hopefully will bring up not just the objective reality of past experiences and future hopes, but also the motivating emotional tag that goes along with that reality. Without good working memory, ADHDers may have difficulty adding emotion to fact, and subsequently may find themselves frustratingly "unmotivated."

In short, then, the ability to modulate behavior comes largely from our pre-frontal lobes, which function primarily as inhibitory centers. Without the luxury of inhibitory brakes, ADHD patients do not get to fully utilize any of their frontal lobe executive functions, either.

What are the different kinds of problems in ADHD?

People with ADHD typically experience problems in three domains: (1) executive function; (2) co-occurring (also called "co-morbid") conditions; and (3) family stresses. Let's look at each domain in more detail. Also, see the important and inspired works by Barkley (2005, 2000), Greene (2005), and Silver (1999).

1. Symptoms of executive dysfunction

In the previous section, we defined the components of executive dysfunction using the terminology of neuropsychologists. Now, let's translate the problems in these areas into real life symptoms.

A. CLASSIC SYMPTOMS OF ADHD

ADHD is typically defined as a triad of inattention, impulsivity, and hyperactivity. Box 2 is a simplified version of the official US DSM-IV criteria for ADHD as defined by the American Psychiatric Association. These are the symptoms that receive the most attention from doctors, and all come from an inability to inhibit.

- Distractible ← inadequate inhibition of external stimuli.
- Impulsive ← inadequate inhibition of internal stimuli.
- Hyperactive ← physically checking out those stimuli.

B. OTHER SYMPTOMS OF EXECUTIVE DYSFUNCTION

If we do not address the additional resulting executive function issues, we are only dealing with the tip of the iceberg. These are not just "incidental" symptoms. They are hard to live with—ask the patient, his family, or his teachers.

Box 2 Simplified DSM-IV criteria for ADHD

Modified and reprinted with permission from the Diagnostic and Statistical Manual of Mental Disorders, Fourth Edition, Text Revision. (Copyright 2000). American Psychiatric Association.

A. Either (1) or (2)

    (1) Six or more symptoms of inattention

        (a) fails to give close attention; makes careless mistakes

        (b) difficulty sustaining attention

        (c) does not seem to listen when spoken to directly

        (h) easily distracted by extraneous stimuli

        (e) difficulty organizing tasks

        (d) fails to follow through (not volitional or incapable)

        (f) avoids tasks requiring sustained organization

        (g) looses things needed for tasks

        (i) often forgetful in daily activities

    (2) Six or more symptoms of hyperactivity-impulsivity

        Hyperactivity

        (a) fidgets/squirms

        (b) leaves seat

        (c) runs or climbs excessively

        (d) difficulty playing in leisure activities quietly

        (e) "on the go" or "driven by a motor"

        (f) talks excessively

        Impulsivity

        (a) blurts out answers before questions completed

        (b) difficulty waiting turn

        (c) interrupts or intrudes

B. Some symptoms present before 7 y.o.

C. Symptoms in two or more settings

D. Interferes with functioning

E. Not exclusively part of other syndrome

The symptoms of disorganization have been grouped together and placed in bold by the author to demonstrate how much disorganization is built into the definition of ADHD.

Using these criteria, DSM-IV defines three subtypes of ADHD:
    ADHD, Predominantly Inattentive Type.
    ADHD, Predominantly Hyperactive-Impulsive Type.
    ADHD, Combined type.

It is essential to recognize that these difficult behaviors are typically built into an ADHDer's life. Otherwise, we will think that we have a child/student with ADHD who incidentally shows horrible self-control, not recognizing that they are all part of the same neurological package of ADHD/executive dysfunction.

☐ Act like moths—attracted to the brightest light. ADHDers are like moths: they are always smack up against the brightest light. Sometimes, the brightest light is a fascinating paperclip on the desk. Sometimes it is the shiny pen. Rarely will the brightest light be a book report that is due in two weeks. Unfortunately, sometimes the brightest light is a bug-zapper (see Figure 3, p.24).

☐ Able to focus on videogames forever, but not on homework. (Dad says, "Don't tell me he has a short attention span!! He plays Nintendo forever.") ADHD doesn't mean that you can't pay attention. It means that you can't pay attention to anything that isn't the most fascinating. Like moths, if you leave ADHDers in front of the most amazing attraction (which for moths are light bulbs, and for boys are anything with a screen), they will stay there—until something else becomes more interesting. When it comes to homework, even a piece of lint might qualify as more intruiging.

☐ Trouble actually executing a task. (Johnny finds himself saying, "I'm gonna do it, I'm gonna do it…Holy cow, I didn't do it.") Most kids with ADHD intend to do their homework. Their trouble actually initiating tasks, though, prevents the execution of the job. They are probably as surprised as anyone when the teacher asks for the homework and they realize they don't have it.

☐ Poor organization. ("Johnny, I can't believe that we spent hours fighting over your homework, and then you couldn't find it when your teacher asked for it!" And, "Why do I have to keep going back to school for your books?")

☐ Inconsistent work and behavior. ("Johnny, if you could do it well yesterday, why is today so horrible?") With 100% of their energy, ADHDers may be able to control the task that most of us can do with 50% of our focus. But who can continually muster 100% effort? As the joke goes: ADHD children do something right once, and we hold it against them for the rest of their lives.

☐ Trouble returning to task. ("Johnny, you never complete anything. You get distracted and don't bother finishing. You just don't care.")

☐ Poor sense of time. ("Johnny, what have you been doing all afternoon? You can't spend one hour on just the first paragraph!")

☐ Time moves too slowly. ("Mommy, this shopping trip is taking forever!")

☐ Lack of foresight!!! ("Johnny, you'll never be prepared for midterms if you spend the weekend playing videogames. Why do you keep shooting yourself in the foot?") Mothers are usually endowed with great foresight—verging on obsession—with their child's future happiness. They are often crushed as they watch their child repeatedly head down counter-productive paths. On any given afternoon, Johnny is angry that his mother won't let him watch television right now, and his mother is already planning Johnny's future divorce and getting fired—because no one else in the future is going to put up with this behavior. Now, Mom could probably calm down a little bit: Johnny will probably still get into college even if he doesn't hand in tomorrow's French homework. However, her ability to predict Johnny's future needs probably is more accurate than her son's. (See Figure 4, p.26 and Figure 5, p.27.)

☐ Poor hindsight/trouble learning from mistakes. ("Johnny, didn't you remember the problems you had on last semester's finals when you didn't get your papers written in advance?") Unable to inhibit the present, Johnny cannot stop to consider lessons from the past.

☐ Live at the "mercy of the moment." ("All Johnny can do is react to whatever is happening to him right then and there.") ADHD behaviors make sense once we realize that they are based on reactions taking only the present moment into account. Johnny does care about the future; he does appreciate all of the nice things that you have done for him in the past. It is just that, right now, the future and the past don't even exist. Such is the nature of the disability. Sorry.

☐ Living by the "Four-Second Rule." If you want to understand and predict an ADHDer's actions, simply ask yourself, "What would you do if you felt like the world was going to end in four seconds?" Really, what would you do? It probably wouldn't be your homework. And not withstanding ethics, if you were caught in a lie—and there was no future reputation to worry about because the world was ending in four seconds—it probably wouldn't be to tell the truth, either.

☐ Poor ability to utilize "self-talk" to work through a problem. ("Johnny, what were you thinking?! Did you ever think this through?")

☐ Poor sense of self-awareness. (Johnny will probably answer the above question, "I don't know." He's probably right. He doesn't know. After all, he never got as far as actually thinking.)

☐ Poor reading of social clues. ("Johnny, can't you see that the other children think that's weird?") Johnny is too overwhelmed to note other people's reactions.

☐ Trouble with transitions. ("Johnny, why do you curse at me when I'm just calling you for dinner?") Poor ability to shift agendas frequently pushes an ADHDer over the edge and into a meltdown.

☐ Hyperfocused at times. ("When Johnny is on the computer, I can't get him off. And once his father gets his mind on something, off he goes!")

☐ Push away those whose help they need the most. ("Mommy, stop checking my assignment pad. Get out!")

☐ Poor frustration tolerance. ("Johnny, why can't you even let me help you get over this?")

☐ Frequently overwhelmed and angry. ("Mommy, just stop. I can't stand it. Just stop. Please!")

- ☐ "Hyper-responsiveness." ("Mommy, you know I hate sprinkles on my donuts! You never do anything for me! I hate you!") Barkley (2000) uses the term hyper-responsiveness to indicate that people with ADHD have excessive emotions. Their responses, however, are appropriate to what they are actually feeling. So next time you see someone "overreacting," realize that they are actually "over-feeling," and must feel really awful at that moment.

- ☐ Inflexible/explosive reactions. ("Johnny, you're stuck on this. No, I can't just leave you alone. Johnny, now you're not thinking clearly.") See Chapter 3 on staying calm.

- ☐ Feels calm only when in motion. ("He always seems happiest when he is busy. Is that why he stays at work so late?")

- ☐ Thrill seeking behavior. ("He feels most 'on top of his game' during an emergency. He seems to crave stimulation at any cost.")

- ☐ Trouble paying attention to others. ("My husband never listens when I talk to him. He just cannot tolerate sitting around with me and the kids. He doesn't 'pay attention' to his family any more than he 'paid attention' in school.") As the ADHDer gets older, people in his life will increasingly expect more time and empathy to be directed their way. Yet, the above behaviors may interfere with the demonstration of these traits.

- ☐ Trouble with mutual exchange of favors with friends. Without establishing a reliable "bank account" of kept promises, friendships can be hard to make and keep.

- ☐ Sense of failure to achieve goals. ("I start projects, but never get back to the details to complete them. Somehow, I never accomplished the things that I could have done.") This deep disappointment is commonly what brings adults with ADHD to seek help.

- ☐ Lying, cursing, stealing, and blaming others become frequent components of ADHD; especially as the child gets older. According to some particularly depressing data by Barkley *et al.* (1990), here is how ADHD children compare to typical children:

- ° 72% of ADHD children argue with adults (vs. 21% of typical children)

- ° 66% of ADHD children blame others for their own mistakes (vs.17% of typical children)

- ° 71% of ADHD children act touchy or easily annoyed (vs. 20% of typical children)

- ° 40% of ADHD children swear (vs. 6% of typical children)

- ° 49% of ADHD children lie (vs. 5% of typical children).

In short, the symptoms of ADHD become less "cute" as the children switch from elementary to secondary schools. The "good" news comes from understanding that these problems are commonly part of the syndrome we call ADHD. They are nobody's fault—not yours, and not your child's. This understanding points the way towards coping with these issues.

The neurological basis of ADHD

If standard US American Psychiatric Association *DSM-IV* criteria are applied, ADHD occurs in roughly 6% of children no matter where in the world we look (Barkley 2000). Although only 6% (i.e., 1 out of 16) children have the condition, it seems even more prevalent. That's because an occurrence in 1 out of 16 people means that roughly one out of four families are affected by the condition (assuming four people per family). Yes, if four mothers get together, then one of their households will be affected by ADHD. That's a lot of families. True ADHD is a biological condition. The current understanding can be summarized as follows:

- The frontal and pre-frontal lobes (conveniently enough, located in the front part of our brain behind the forehead) are the home of our executive and inhibitory functions.

- In ADHD, there is insufficient action in these areas by the neurotransmitters dopamine and norepinephrine.

- People with ADHD thus show poor executive and inhibitory behaviors.

Simply put, in ADHD, the frontal lobe brakes are asleep on the job. As explained in Chapter 6 on medications, stimulant medications work by increasing dopamine and norepinephrine levels, thus waking up the frontal lobe brakes. ADHD and its treatment are the subjects of thousands of scientific studies. Adoption and other genetic studies, epidemiological studies, MRI studies, fMRI studies, EEG studies, and PET scans all combine to give frankly incontrovertible evidence for the existence of this medical condition and the effectiveness of current treatments. Smith *et al.* (2006) review some of this research in ADHD:

- SPECT (single-photon emission computed tomography) shows decreased blood flow to the prefrontal regions (especially on the right).

- PET (positron emission tomography) scans show diminished glucose metabolism in adult frontal lobes.

- MRI (magnetic resonance imaging) scans show smaller anterior right frontal regions, along with smaller size of the cerebellar vermis and some of the basal ganglia to which they connect.

- fMRI (functional MRI) scans show abnormality in the same regions when ADHD children attend or inhibit.

- EEGs (electroencephalograms) show frontal lobe slowing and excessive beta activity (indicative of under-arousal of the frontal lobes).

- Twin studies show that genetic factors control up to 75 to 97% of a person's risk for ADHD.

- Psychological tests show poor working memory and other executive functions.

- Biological factors in the environment associated with ADHD include lead exposure, prematurity at birth, low birth weight, and prenatal exposure to alcohol and tobacco.

In 1998, the American Medical Association concluded that ADHD has been one of the best-researched medical conditions, and that evidence for its validity are much more compelling than the evidence for most mental conditions and even many medical disorders (Goldman *et al.* 1998). Further, Smith *et al.* (2006, p.73, 76) conclude that based on research: "purely social causes of ADHD can be largely ruled out as likely contributors to most forms of ADHD...Studies consistently find little if any effect for shared (rearing) environment on the traits of ADHD; this refutes an effort to attribute ADHD to poor parenting, family diet, household television exposure, or other popularly held causes for the disorder." In general, the only "blame" for these behaviors that you can pin on the parents is the contribution of their genes—but they didn't have much choice in that.

2. Co-occurring disorders associated with ADHD

In addition to the neurologically-based executive dysfunctions above, there are myriad co-occurring disorders that frequently accompany the diagnosis of ADHD in the patient and/or her family. These disorders may often be misdiagnosed as ADHD, may co-occur with ADHD, or may exacerbate the ADHD. In addition, many people are "subsyndromal," and have just parts of the following diagnoses. Ratey and Johnson (1998) refer to these as "shadow syndromes." The presence of these other disorders should be investigated whenever the diagnosis of ADHD is being considered.

This information does not constitute medical advice. Medication use in children is frequently done "off-label," and information is often quite limited. Not all of the medications discussed in this text have U.S. Food and Drug Administration approval for children, or for some of the indications that they are commonly used for. Recommendations need to be taken as subject to change and debate. See Chapter 6 on medications. This information is not intended to be all-inclusive; and full discussion of the usefulness, side effects, risks, monitoring, drug interactions, etc. of these medications is beyond this book. Check with your doctor, the package insert, and www.FDA.gov for new and complete information. The reader is also referred to *ADHD with Comorbid Disorders* by Pliszka *et al.* (1999), which forms much of the basis for the following medication assessments. Medical treatment of the associated disorders is perhaps best done in consultation with a neurologist or psychiatrist.

A. LEARNING DISABILITIES (LD)

Brown (2005) concludes that 70% of children with ADHD have a learning disability. A review of the diagnostic criteria for ADHD (Box 2, p.136) will show that a disability in the area of organization is virtually built into the syndrome of ADHD by definition. Following directions, sequencing problems and dysgraphia are also particularly common. Learning disabilities should be suspected whenever a student does not "live up to his or her potential." They are identified with history, exam and psycho-educational testing. As well explained by Larry Silver (1999), learning disabilities can either exacerbate or mimic ADHD. After all, how long can someone focus on something that she does not understand?

B. DISRUPTIVE BEHAVIORAL DISORDERS

More than 50% of ADHD children meet criteria for a disruptive behavioral disorder (MTA Cooperative Group 1999). Even in the absence of a full diagnosis, the lives of many (if not most) children with ADHD are afflicted by lying, cursing, taking things that do not belong to them, blaming others, and being easily angered. This frequency is not surprising given the executive dysfunction hypothesis. Full definitions of the disruptive behavioral disorders can be found in the Diagnostic and Statistical Manual-IV American Psychiatric Association (2000). Medications such as Depakote (valproic acid), Catapres (clonidine), Tenex (guanfacine), and Risperdal (risperidone) can sometimes help with impulsivity and aggression. The three conditions that comprise behavioral disorders are:

- Oppositional defiant disorder (ODD). Whereas ADHD children are not able to comply because of inattention or impulsivity, ODD children are unwilling to conform (even with an intriguing task). They may be deliberately negative, annoying, belligerent, angry or spiteful. Although many children with ADHD and mood disorders meet diagnostic criteria for ODD, I personally rarely diagnose the latter condition, instead finding most of the negative behaviors as inadvertently stemming from an overwhelmed nervous system that is facing as yet unsolved problems.

- Conduct disorder (CD). Children with CD are more frequently overtly hostile and law breaking, with a lack of remorse that is not seen in ADHD alone. These people violate the rights of others, such as with physical cruelty to others or animals, stealing, etc.

- Antisocial personality disorder. People with antisocial personality disorder have a pervasive pattern of severe violation of the rights of others, typically severe enough to merit arrest.

C. ANXIETY DISORDER

Anxiety disorder occurs in 34% of children with ADHD (MTA Cooperative Group 1999), but half of these children never tell their parents (Bernstein and Layne 2004)! Patients are beset most days by painful, unwelcome worries not due to any imminent stressor. Children may appear edgy, stressed out, tense, sleepless, or have panic attacks. Treatments include the following:

- Change of environment, exercise, and meditation.

- Cognitive behavioral therapy (CBT) should be tried, if available.

- SSRIs (selective serotonin reuptake inhibitors) such as Prozac, etc.

- Buspar (buspirone)—helps anxiety but not panic attacks.

- Klonopin (clonazepam)—helps anxiety.

- Tricyclics—help some with anxiety, and work well for panic attacks.

- Stimulants may directly worsen anxiety, but may help indirectly if the anxiety was created by issues related to inattention.

D. OBSESSIVE COMPULSIVE DISORDER (OCD)

Recurrent and intrusive obsessive thoughts, and compulsive actions (which are done in an effort to neutralize those thoughts) may occur in up to one-third of ADHD patients (Geller *et al.* 1996). If ADHD is living in the present, then anxiety/OCD is living in the future. Although difficult to live with, the future goal directed behavior of anxiety/OCD may help overcome the organizational problems of ADHD. Cognitive behavioral therapy (CBT) should be tried first, if available. SSRIs (such as Prozac) are the current mainstay of medical treatment.

E. MAJOR DEPRESSION

Estimates for the co-occurrence of ADHD and depression are 15 to 75% of ADHD children and 47% of ADHD adults (Brown 2005). Although pure ADHD patients get depressed briefly, they flow with the environment (changing within minutes). In contrast, depressed children stay depressed for long periods. The symptoms include loss of joy, sadness, pervasive irritability (not just in response to specific frustrations), withdrawal, self-critical outlook, and vegetative symptoms (abnormal sleep or appetite). Treatment includes:

- counseling and adjustment of the environment

- selective serotonin uptake inhibitors (SSRIs) such as Prozac (fluoxetine)

- Wellbutrin (bupropion), which helps depression and ADHD

- tricyclics (e.g., Tofranil and Pamelor) do not appear to work for depression in children.

F. BIPOLAR DEPRESSION

Bipolar depression occurs in up to 16% of ADHD children (Pliszka *et al.* 1999). In one word, these patients are "extreme!" Bipolar patients classically show depression cycling with abnormally elevated, expansive, grandiose, and pressured moods. Children may cycle within hours. Other hallmarks include severe separation anxiety, often precociousness as children, extreme irritability, extreme rages that last for hours, very goal directed behavior, and little sleep requirement. They may demonstrate hypersexuality, gory dreams, extreme fear of death, extreme sensitivity to stimuli, often oppositional or obsessive traits, heat intolerance, craving for sweets, bedwetting, hallucinations, possible suicidal tendencies, or substance abuse. Often symptoms are shown only at home (see *The Bipolar Child* by Papolos and Papolos 2006). Consider bipolar when a diagnosis of "ADHD" is accompanied by the above symptoms or the following:

- Family history of bipolar disorder, substance abuse, or suicide.

- Prolonged temper tantrums and mood swings. Sometimes the angry, violent, mean, and disorganized outbursts last for hours (vs. less then 30 minutes in ADHD). Also, bipolar rages are typically from parental limit setting; in ADHD, rages are from overstimulation.

- Oppositional/defiant behaviors.

- Explosive and "intentionally" aggressive or risk-seeking behavior.

- Substance abuse.

- Separation anxiety, bad dreams, disturbed sleep, or fascination with gore.

- Morning irritability which lasts hours (vs. minutes in ADHD).

- Symptoms worsen with stimulants or typical antidepressants.

Medical treatments of bipolar depression include:

- valproate (Depakote)

- carbamazepine (Tegretol) clearly helps bipolar and aggressive symptoms at least in adults (not as well studied in children)

- lithium (which may not work as well in ultra-rapid cyclers)

- plus risperidone (Risperdal) for psychotic symptoms and aggression.

Note: stimulants and antidepressants may trigger mania and worsen bipolar depression.

G. TICS AND TOURETTE'S (MOTOR AND VOCAL TICS)

Seven percent of ADHD children have tics; but 60% of Tourette's patients have ADHD (Waslick and Greenhill 2004). Briefly defined, Tourette's is marked by long periods of at least one vocal tic (such as throat clearing or sniffling), and at least two motor tics (such as eye blinking or neck stretching). The first line of treatment is reassurance and not drawing attention to the tics. Medical treatments should be considered if the tics become socially disabling. Medications for tics include clonidine (Catapres) and guanfacine (Tenex), which help impulsivity and tics. Risperidone (Risperdal) and other neuroleptics are quite helpful. Note that stimulants may exacerbate (or sometimes be associated with improvement of) tics. Streptococcus and other infections may sometimes lead to an exacerbation of tics and/or anxiety/OCD in a condition called PANDAS (Pediatric Autoimmune Neuropsychiatric Disorders Associated with Strep).

H. ASPERGER'S SYNDROME

Attwood (2007) concludes that 75% of people with Asperger's syndrome have ADHD. Symptoms of Asperger's include impaired ability to utilize social cues such as body language, irony, or other "subtext" of communication; restricted eye contact and socialization; limited range of encyclopedic interests; perseverative, odd behaviors; didactic, monotone voice; "concrete" thinking; oversensitivity to certain stimuli; and unusual movements. See Attwood's (2007) recent book on Asperger's syndrome.

I. SENSORY INTEGRATION (SI) DYSFUNCTION

SI dysfunction (also now called "sensory processing disorder," SPD) is the inability to process information received through the senses at the right "volume" level. The child may be either oversensitive or undersensitive to stimuli. Or, the child may not be able to execute a coordinated response to the stimuli. SI may mimic or coexist with ADHD. SI is typically evaluated by an occupational therapist. See Kranowitz's (1998) book for more information. Some types of SI include:

- hypersensitive to touch: sensitive to clothes or getting dirty; withdraw to light kiss

- hyposensitive to touch: wallow in mud; rub against things; unaware of pain

- hypersensitive to movement: avoid running, climbing, or swinging

- hyposensitive to movement: rocking; twirling; unusual positions

- may also respond abnormally to sights, sounds, smells, tastes, or textures

- may be clumsy, have trouble coordinating (bilateral) movements; or have poor fine motor skills.

J. CENTRAL AUDITORY PROCESSING DISORDER (CAPD)

Central auditory processing refers to the steps taken by the brain to convert sounds into meaning. Symptoms of CAPD include trouble with comprehension of information presented through the ears, following a sequence of directions, following long conversations, tolerating noise, and worsened comprehension when faced with competing sounds. CAPD frequently co-occurs with ADHD. To further confuse matters, CAPD shares some symptoms with ADHD, such as trouble concentrating, trouble filtering out the background, and trouble following a sequence of directions. Detailed testing is done through specialized audiology evaluations.

3. Familial issues

These can be of two categories:

A. FAMILY MEMBERS WITH THEIR OWN NEURO-PSYCHIATRIC PROBLEMS

Family members may have their own ADHD, OCD, depression, anxiety, etc. In fact, a child with ADHD has a 40% chance that one of his parents has ADHD (Kutscher *et al.* 2005). Such difficulties affect the family's ability to cope with the ADHD child, and may need to be addressed independently.

B. STRESS—CREATED BY THE CHILD—CYCLING BACK TO FURTHER CHALLENGE THE PATIENT

Children or adults with ADHD can create chaos throughout the entire family, stressing everyone in the process. The morning routine and homework are frequent (and lengthy!) sources of dissension. Other siblings are often resentful of the time and special treatment given to the ADHD child. Mothers, who frequently consider their child's homework to be their own, find it stressful that "their" homework never seems to get completed. Fathers come home to discover a family in distress, and that they are expected to deal not only with a child who is out of control, but also with the mother who is understandably now losing it, too. Parents may argue over the "best strategy," a difficult problem since few strategies are even close to perfect. The unpleasantness of life around someone with ADHD leads to a pattern of avoidance, which only furthers the cycle of anger. In turn, all of this family turmoil creates a new source of pressures and problems for the already stressed ADHD patient to deal with. The last thing that an overwhelmed ADHD child needs is a stressed out mother or father!

Non-medical treatments for ADHD

First, we need to identify and treat any of the above co-occurring conditions. Next, we need to recognize that "ADHD" is shorthand for the entire biologically-based spectrum that was just discussed. Otherwise, parents will think that they have a child with ADHD who just also happens to be difficult and/or appear mean spirited. Now, the good news: There are truly effective (albeit not instantaneous) ways to improve the lives of the ADHD child and her caregivers. These non-medical approaches can be simplified to four basic principles:

1. Keep it positive.
2. Keep it calm.
3. Keep it organized.
4. Keep it going.

Rule #1: Keep it positive

Keep it positive. It seems obvious enough. After all, it is the rare person whose attitude is improved by constant criticism. Yet after years of frustration and unmet expectations, family life may have deteriorated to a life of sarcasm, putdowns, or arguments. Families may need some specific mindsets and techniques to get things on an upswing. Here they are.

Get "a kick" out of your child

At this point in your life, enjoying your child may seem like a long-lost idea. It's okay to be a little (or even a lot) frustrated, as long as you still get "a kick" out of your child's unique qualities. Maintain a sense of humor! Seek to enjoy, not to be frustrated. Celebrate the child's humor, creativity, passion, and "Why not?" attitude. These are amazing kids, even if they don't quite fit the mold of most people on planet Earth. Laugh with each other. It's never too late to let your child make you smile, even if you're just chuckling warmly in disbelief.

If a child's basic relationship with her parents is so full of anger and resentment that she no longer finds pride in pleasing her parents, then those basic relationships need some healing first. Set aside a period of special time (up to 30 minutes) where the goal is simply to exist together pleasantly in the same room. The child gets to choose the (reasonable) activity, and the parent gets to enjoy being near their child without provoking a world war. Avoid saying anything critical—even if it would be helpful. Keep questions and comments (even positive ones) to a minimal level. After all, any interruption is still annoying. The goal here is to put your account of good/bad interactions into a positive balance, making it more likely for the child to want to please you. That sets the stage for smoother discipline in the future. Dr. Russell Barkley (2005) and Dr. David Rabiner (2006) provide a full explanation of behavior modification techniques.

Figure out "Why did he do that?"

Ask yourself, "Why did he do that?" There is always a reason, even if it does not appear rational, even if it causes the child to be shooting himself in his own foot, and even if the child himself is not aware of the reason for his behavior.

Maintain a disability outlook

Perhaps oddly enough, considering your child as having a disability (Barkley 2000) is a way to keep things positive. If you insist that there is no disability in self-control, then you are likely to conclude that your child is willfully disobedient. If you insist that your child has no problem with organization and foresight, then you will conclude that your child chooses to simply not care. A disability outlook helps the caregiver to empathize, and also helps remove blame (although the child will still be stuck with the results of his behavior).

Don't take the difficult behaviors as personal affronts

The answer to the question, "Why can't he be like all of the other children?" is that he can't. It isn't personal. You just happen to be the person in the room. Parents need to see themselves as "therapists" for their problematic child—not as victims of him. Always remember that there is a real, live child underneath all of those problems. It may also help to remember that the person who suffers most from these behaviors is usually the child himself. These children sabotage themselves just as often as they bother anyone else. What further evidence could we have that these problems are not fully within their control?

Minimize frustrations by taking a realistic look at the child you get every day

Phelan (1994) suggests that a realistic assessment of your child's starting point helps minimize your anger and frustration with her when she doesn't live up to what you would like. Periodically, take stock of who is showing up in your life everyday. This is your starting point. Not a typical child. This is what you can likely expect today.

Forgive yourself daily

Dr. Barkley (2000) urges his readers to forgive themselves nightly for their inability to be perfect. Each night, review how you've done that day and how you could do it better. Then, remember that each of us is only human, and forgive yourself for these past imperfections. This applies to parents, children, and teachers.

Keep your relational bank account in the positive

It may help to consider that you have a bank account of experiences with the child: there are good times and bad times that can be deposited into your relationship. Your goal is to have the overall balance be in the positive. As you enter into each interaction, ask yourself, "Will my next comment/action make my bank account with the child run into debt or into a positive flow?"

Keep it positive by redirecting before the problem occurs

When things start going badly, redirect to a positive direction—rather than criticizing the misbehavior after it occurs. For example, if the child is just beginning to fight with her sister, then redirect/distract to a new activity, rather than hand out a punishment after the big fight occurs. In this way, you might replace an afternoon of screaming with a trip to the ice cream parlor.

Ensure success by providing help for deficits at the moment it is needed

Keep things successful and positive for children with special difficulties by enabling at the time of need, not by handing out negative feedback when it is already too late. Unfortunately, the simple reality is that negative consequences do not usually teach the needed behaviors to kids with disabilities. Typically, they know what to do; they just cannot carry out the plan (Barkley 2000).

Provide a safety net

Let's try an analogy. When acrobats are taught a new trapeze act, their trainers provide them with a safety net. No one worries that providing these safeguards will interfere with learning, or will make the performer take his task less seriously. It is simply that, without a safety net, the penalty for missing a handgrip while flying across the trapeze bars is neither commensurate with the mistake, nor productive. Be the safety net or "spotter" for the special needs kid. If she gets it right, she won't need you, and there's no harm done that you were standing by. If she doesn't get it right, you are there to provide a softer landing—and make sure that the consequence is appropriate to the mistake (see Figure 9, p.105).

Don't be a nasty cop

Dr. Joseph Carver (2005) asks you to imagine being pulled over by a policeman for making an illegal turn. The policeman approaches your window, hands you the ticket, and proceeds to insult you. What would you think about the policeman? Moral of the story: as you hand out the punishment, skip the nasty attitude. The punishment is bad enough. The nasty attitude just breeds resentment.

Minimize arguments with the "no-fault" approach

Zeigler Dendy (2006) has the very useful suggestion that rules be enforced with a no-fault approach. In other words, avoid arguments based on whose fault it is. Just deal with the end results. For example, it doesn't matter why a child arrives home late. She is late, this is the consequence, and this is the plan to prevent it from happening again. It really simplifies discussion, doesn't it?

Punishment is not your chance to inflict misery: it is your chance to improve your child's upcoming decisions

The purpose of a punishment presumably is to correct future behaviors. A modest, immediate punishment is likely to be at least as effective as a prolonged one. A spiral of increasing punishments is unlikely to work, and just saddles everyone with a prolonged period of unhappiness in the future. So, when punishment is required, keep it immediate and controlled. Better yet, teach the skills needed to avoid the negative behavior in the first place—especially since punishment is not typically effective for children with ADHD.

Avoid the "resentment treadmill"

The endless cycle of mutual resentment leads nowhere good. Everyone can agree to that. Someone has to get off the treadmill first. It isn't going to be the dysfunctional child. That leaves the mature adult to take the first leap. (That's you.) Don't expect instant results or gratitude (Kutscher *et al.* 2005).

If it's not actually useful, don't do it

Amazingly, many of us keep using the same "useless" or harmful strategies over and over again, as if they might magically work on the four hundred and first try. An unproductive chide or ineffective command may make you feel better for two seconds, but won't improve your child's life—or your relationship with her. So why do it? Seriously.

Avoid the "four cardinal sins"

Thomas Phelan (1994) identifies the "four cardinal sins." These "sins" are ineffective and actually harmful. Why would we use them? Instead, either (a) decide that the issue is aggravating but not significant enough to warrant intervention (i.e., stay quiet); or (b) schedule an appointment with your child to discuss the issue. The "four cardinal sins" to avoid are:

1. Don't nag. It hasn't worked yet. If you don't have anything nice to say, don't say it. Even simple comments like "How was your day?" may cause frustration in some children.

2. Don't lecture. It doesn't work either. Plus, given their sense of time, ADHDers will find the experience interminable. Instead, give one or two brief, clear instructions. "Insight transplants" from you to your child, as Phelan calls them, are unlikely to work.

3. Don't offer unscheduled, spontaneous "advice." What are the odds that your Nintendo playing teen will respond pleasantly to your request to discuss right now that book report due in two weeks?

4. Don't argue. It takes two to fight. No argument can occur without your permission.

Be patient: this is the 50-year plan

Don't expect that all problems can be fixed overnight. Many of these kids will be working on their issues as part of a "50-year plan." In the meantime, remember that threats may change behavior, but they do not produce a good attitude. Only success and rewards (internal or external) can do that. Give it time. This is not war. We are all on the same team.

Remember that some of the difficult child/adolescent behavior is simply normal

We may be quick to pin all difficult moments with the child as being due to some "disorder." Keep in mind, though, that life with any child is never totally smooth. Every family up and down the street, and every teacher up and down the hallway, is having some problems as well. That may be comforting. Misery loves company.

Rule #2: Keep it calm

Some people's brains have poor frustration tolerance and are too inflexible. Nothing good can come from a "discussion" held by out of control people (see Figure 7, p.71). Once that fact is recognized, some families may be ready for Plan B: try to prevent incoherent "meltdowns" before they occur, by a process Ross Greene (2005) calls "Collaborative Problem Solving." This is essentially a three-step approach:

1. The child puts his concerns on the table, and the adult empathizes with those concerns.

2. The adult puts his concerns on the table.

3. The child is invited to start the negotiation process towards a doable, win–win solution to 1 and 2.

It is best if these negotiations occur well in advance of the heated moments. However, if there is an impending meltdown, allow a cooling off period at the first signs. Once cool heads prevail all around, calm discussion of the issue can ensue productively. An attitude of negotiation must prevail on all sides. Sometimes, we are better off just "picking our fights." These approaches are empathically explained in Ross W. Greene's excellent book, *The Explosive Child* (2005).

In summary, *stop!!!* Remember, the hallmark of ADHD is trouble stopping—trouble putting on the brakes. Thus, it is not surprising that the first step in dealing with ADHD is to *stop*. Only then can executive function resurface. Typically, when calm and unthreatened, even the ADHD brain will make the correct choice. The need to first *stop* applies to both the child and us! (See Figure 6, p.69 and Figure 8, p.72.)

Rule #3: Keep it organized
Disorganization is virtually built into the definition of ADHD

Organization is the holy grail for ADHDers, as virtually all people with ADHD are innately disorganized. In fact, if we rearrange the diagnostic criteria for the inattentive type of ADHD, we see that five of the nine criteria are purely organizational—and you only need six criteria to qualify.

Don't confuse disorganization with "he doesn't care"

Indeed, a child with ADHD might fight with his parents for hours as he muddles through his homework, and then he might actually forget to hand it in! ADHDers don't have typically functioning brains in the area of organization. Their brain may be extremely capable in the area of writing an English paper, but extremely poor in the area of organization required to find it the next morning. This striking unevenness in skills is what makes the organizational problem a disability.

"Sink or swim" does not work for kids with disabilities

Do we think that demoralizing deductions will teach him organizational skills, any more than punishment would teach a child with dyslexia how to read? If punishment was going to work for this child, it should have been working a long time ago. It didn't, and it won't. Why? Because these kids can't swim yet when left to their own abilities. If they could, they would have. Do we really think that these kids choose to do poorly?

Remember, kids with ADHD have trouble executing the skills that they have learned. As Barkley (2000) puts it, they have trouble doing what they know, not trouble knowing what to do. For example, they already know to write down all of their assignments, and to hand them in on time. It's just that their poor executive function skills don't allow them to execute those skills. So, we need to provide a safety net by constantly supervising that they have used the organizational skills that we teach them.

Don't worry that we'll be making their lives too easy. Even with our understanding and support, these kids will still suffer more frustration and setbacks than the average student. We should only wish that our interventions were so successful that ADHDers' lives will now be easier than everyone else's.

Teacher/parent communication in "real-time" is essential

In order to provide the ADHD child with the necessary organizational safety net, it is essential that teachers stay in close contact with the parents. Use phone calls. Use email. But stay in touch! Mid-term progress notes come too late to do anything with the information. Don't expect the ADHD child to be a reliable link in this communication chain between teachers and parents.

The five major components of an organizational system

Not surprisingly, then, accommodations for an ADHD child's disorganization need to be a major part of school plans for ADHD. There are five principle elements required to keep a student organized:

1. An assignment pad. Alas, most kids with ADHD don't have the executive functions to know where the pad is located, no less

to actually use it every day for every subject. This is where surrogate frontal lobes come in—harmlessly donated by the classroom teacher, skills teacher, and parents. Teachers, please come around and check that the ADHD students are actually writing down their assignments! Do not wait for the student to come to you for your initials. If they were organized enough to do that, they would not have needed this accommodation in the first place.

2. A monthly planner. Question: how do you plan for the long-term projects? Answer: you record them on a monthly calendar. For example, if a book report is due in two weeks, have your child write it down on the monthly calendar. Then, work with the student to break down the project and record the due dates for the multiple steps involved in the project, such as when to get the book, read the book, write the rough draft, edit it, and hand in the report. Remember, time is very vague to someone with ADHD. Make it visually tangible with the planner.

3. A bi-fold folder for all papers coming from school (left side) and going back to school (right side). On the left side of the pocket goes every piece of paper that has the child's fingerprints on it from today. If Johnny has touched it, it goes there. At home, the papers can be put into their proper place, under careful surrogate lobe supervision if needed. On the right pocket of the bi-fold go all papers that are due to be handed in tomorrow. When the math teacher asks for the homework, there is only one place it could be—in that right pocket. And we know that it's there because the surrogate frontal lobes provided a double-check safety net the night before. Remember, this bi-fold gets taken to every class. It's the student version of in/out boxes.

4. A single binder (or two). A single binder—or perhaps one for the morning and one for the afternoon—would work best for ADHD kids. Too many binders means too many hiding places for papers.

5. Most importantly, frontal lobes to supervise use of the above. Surrogate frontal lobes will be required for the next few (say, 50 or so?) years to ensure that the above stuff is actually used. For now, the day that someone stops providing a safety net that the child is actually performing these steps will likely be the day that organization falls apart.

Each day, convert assignment pads into time schedules

Convert the daily and monthly assignments into a time schedule for today—a "To Do" list. Look over the planner—including upcoming weeks—and write out the times that you are going to actually accomplish tasks today. This provides a reality check for what can and cannot be crammed into one day. Note that what you are planning to actually accomplish today may not correlate exactly with what is on today's assignment pad.

Allow the child to make up missed work expediently

If a major deduction for lateness were going to work, it would have been working already. If deduction for lateness actually works to correct the problem, then keep doing it. If not, recognize the problem as a disability that is currently unable to be completely corrected. In such a case, the work does need to be completed, but is not fair for a persistent organizational disability to cause excessive and demoralizing academic deductions. Use one of two methods:

- Accept work handed in within one day of student *and* parental notification of the missing assignment.

- Alternatively, a non-punitive school detention can be assigned during which the child gets the work done, and it is then accepted.

If, for some reason, it is necessary to give an "F," give a grade of 65, not zero. Mathematically, it is virtually impossible to dig out of a zero.

Look for problems associated with the ADHD

Of kids with ADHD, 70% have some other disability. Many of them, in particular, have problems with following directions, following a sequence of directions, written expression, spelling, and handwriting. Use of a laptop/word processor can be of great benefit.

Rule #4: Keep it going

Rule #4 is simple to state but hard to accomplish: keep it going. In other words, keep doing Rules #1–3. ADHDers are born with a neurologically different brain (see the biological findings in Chapter 1). Since this neurologically-based problem is not going away this week, we have two choices: keep providing help for the deficits of ADHD before the kids make mistakes, or keep punishing the child after he makes the mistakes.

Once we understand that negative reinforcement after the fact has not been working (it hasn't yet, has it?), we are ready to provide relief for their disabilities by guiding them at the moment guidance is needed—rather than continued disbelief that they did it wrong again. And when the interventions are working, don't confuse the success of those interventions with a lack of need for them. Keep up your safety net.

Medication treatments for ADHD

When behavioral approaches are insufficient, medication is frequently warranted; and in fact, often gives the patient the tools to successfully follow behavioral plans. Medications for ADHD usually involve the stimulation of frontal lobe function. Remember, the frontal lobes function primarily by way of inhibition. Thus, to use an analogy, stimulants "slow you down" by equipping the bicycle with adequate brakes. Importantly, they do not work by "gumming up the gears." ADHD patients who take medication bump into trouble less often because they are now a high performance bike capable of appropriate braking, not because they are too tired to get going. Like coffee, stimulant medications allow the child to put on the brakes against distractions, impulsivity, overreactions, and frustrations. They give the executive functions a fighting chance (see Figure 10, p.111).

Stimulants

Stimulant medications are the mainstay of medical treatment for ADHD. No other class of medicine works as well or as safely. Although usually well tolerated, the most common side effects are insomnia, loss of appetite, and rebound irritability. Precipitation of behavioral changes, tics, headaches, abdominal distress, questionable possible cardiac and other less common side effects can also occur. The major stimulants are:

- methylphenidate (Ritalin, Concerta, and Metadate CD. Focalin is solely the d-isomer of methylphenidate)

- dextro-amphetamine (Dexedrine)

- mixed amphetamine salts (Adderall and Adderall XR)

- pemoline (Cylert), which is used now rarely because of potential hepatotoxicity.

Non-stimulants

Non-stimulant medications used for ADHD include:

- atomoxetine (Strattera)
  - newer, once daily norepinephrine reuptake inhibitor
  - may be especially useful in patients with tics, anxiety, or insomnia
  - possible rare effects on the liver, the heart, mania, or thoughts of self-harm.
- bupropion (Wellbutrin)
  - novel antidepressant with dopamine and noradrenergic effects
  - may decrease hyperactivity and aggression and improve cognition
  - may precipitate seizures, tics, mania, or thoughts of self-harm.
- nortriptyline (Pamelor) or imipramine (Tofranil)

- cardiac concerns exist regarding their safety

- consider if stimulants are ineffective, or in patients with co-occurring tics

- does not help any co-occurring depression in children in clinical studies, and may possibly bring out thoughts of self-harm).

- clonidine (Catapres) or guanfacine (Tenex)

  - centrally acting alpha-adrenergic agonists

  - help impulsivity/aggression and tics but less useful for attention

  - controversy over apparent safety when used with stimulants; may be sedating; sometimes used at night to combat insomnia.

Top principles

1. Keep it positive. Get a kick out of your child. Keep a sense of humor. Seek to enjoy, not to scream.

2. Celebrate the ADHD person's humor, creativity, and passion.

3. Hate ADHD, not the person with it.

4. You do not have a standard child. You can view ADHD as a wonderful uniqueness. Simultaneously, you can view the issue as a disability. The "disability outlook" will help because it eliminates blame; sets reasonable expectations (thereby minimizing anger), and points the way for parents/teachers to see themselves as "therapists" not victims.

5. Recognize that attention issues in the child are only the tip of the iceberg that everyone must address.

6. The "patient" in ADHD is the whole family and school.

7. Remember that children with ADHD have two time frames: "Now!" and "Huh?" There is no future. There is no past. There is only now.

8. Do you want to understand the ADHDers' actions? Just ask yourself: "What behavior would make sense if you only had four seconds to live?"

9. Instead of punishing wrong behavior, set a reward for the correct behavior you would rather replace it with. Rewards should be immediate, frequent, powerful, clearly defined, and consistent.

10. Plan ahead. Give warnings before transitions. Discuss in advance what is expected. Have the child repeat out loud the terms he just agreed to.

11. Don't argue, nag, lecture, or attempt unsolicited and spontaneous transplants of your wisdom to your child. Instead, either (a) decide that the issue is aggravating but not significant enough to warrant intervention; or (b) make an appointment with your child to discuss the issue.

12. Keep it calm! Head off big fights before they begin. Seek to defuse, not to inflame. When tempers flare, allow everyone to cool off. Serious discussion can only occur during times of composure.

13. Especially with teens, negotiate, negotiate, and negotiate. Parents need to model negotiation, not inflexibility. Don't worry about losing control: the parent always gets to decide when negotiation is over and which compromise is accepted. Remember: negative behaviors usually occur because the ADHDer is spinning out of control, not because he is evil. While evil behavior would need to be aggressively squelched, the much more common overwhelmed behavior needs to calmly defused.

14. Pick your fights. Is the issue at hand worth chipping away at your relationship with your child? Can your child really control the offending behavior at this moment? Although it is not the child's "fault," he will still ultimately be the one to take the consequences of his behavior.

15. Keep it organized!

16. This is hard work.

17. You will make it through this: you have no choice.

18. "The children who need love the most will always ask for it in the most unloving ways." (Words of a teacher quoted by Russell Barkley 2000.)

19. If it is working, keep doing it. If not, do something else.

20. Barkley (2000) implores you to forgive your child and yourself nightly. You didn't ask to live with the effects of ADHD any more than did your child.

21. Review this text, and others, periodically. You are going to forget this stuff, and different principles will likely be needed at different stages. A good way to remember to review is by subscription to some of the free monthly newsletters on ADHD (see Appendix 3, resources).

22. Steven Covey (2000) suggests imagining your child delivering your eulogy. What do you want him to say about you? Keep those bigger goals in mind as you choose your interactions/reactions to your child.

23. This is not a contest with your child. The winner is not the one with more points. The winner is the one whose child still loves them when they graduate from high school.

Conclusion: "Doctor, will it all be OK?"

In summary, we miss the point when we address only the triad of inattention, impulsivity, and hyperactivity. These symptoms are only the tip of the iceberg. Much greater problems have usually been plaguing the family, but often no one has understood that the associated symptoms described above are part and parcel of the same neurologically-based condition. Without this recognition, families have thought that their ADHD child also was "incidentally" uncooperative and apparently self-absorbed. Unless we recognize that these extended symptoms are part of the same spectrum, parents will not mention them; and doctors will never deal with them.

Given all of this, it is reasonable to ask: "Will this go away?" Personally, I would rephrase the question as, "Will it be OK?" The answer can be "yes," but we must recognize that this is often the "50-year plan." In other words, these children can be wonderfully successful adults, while they continue to work on these issues over their lifetime. Meanwhile, we "just" need to patiently steer them in the positive direction.

Finally, we must also keep in mind that some of the iceberg is fantastic and enviable. While the rest of us are obsessing about the future, or morosing about the past, people with ADHD are experiencing the present. ADHDers can be a lot of fun; dullness is never a problem. Their "Why not?" attitude may free them to take chances that the rest of us may be afraid to take. Their flux of ideas may lead to creative innovations. And most importantly, their extreme passion can be a source of inspiration and accomplishment to the benefit of us all. It's going to be quite a ride, but enjoy it. Then, we're all winners (Figure 11).

Figure 11: Enjoy the ride with your ADHD child!

Behavioral Checklist

Child's Name: _ _ _ _ _ _ _ _ _ _ _   Your Name: _ _ _ _ _ _ _ _ _ _ _ _ _

Date: _ _ _/_ _ _/_ _ _ _   Subject (if teacher): _ _ _ _ _ _ _ _ _

Please rate the severity of each problem listed   Comments
0 = none   1 = slight   2 = moderate   3 = major

	0	1	2	3
Easily distracted	☐	☐	☐	☐
Requires one-to-one attention to get work done	☐	☐	☐	☐
Impulsive (trouble waiting turn, blurts out answers)	☐	☐	☐	☐
Hyperactive (fidgety, trouble staying seated)	☐	☐	☐	☐
Disorganized	☐	☐	☐	☐
Does not write down assignments	☐	☐	☐	☐
Backpack is a mess	☐	☐	☐	☐
Poor sense of time	☐	☐	☐	☐
Over-reacts	☐	☐	☐	☐
Easily overwhelmed	☐	☐	☐	☐
Blows up easily	☐	☐	☐	☐
Trouble switching activities	☐	☐	☐	☐
Poor handwriting	☐	☐	☐	☐
Certain academic tasks seem difficult (specify)	☐	☐	☐	☐
Anxious, edgy, stressed, or painfully worried	☐	☐	☐	☐

	0	1	2	3
Obsessive thoughts or fears; perseverative rituals	☐	☐	☐	☐
Seems deliberately spiteful, cruel or annoying	☐	☐	☐	☐
Irritated for hours or days on end (not just frequent, brief blow-ups)	☐	☐	☐	☐
Depressed, "empty," sad, or unhappy	☐	☐	☐	☐
Extensive mood swings	☐	☐	☐	☐
Tics: repetitive movements or noises	☐	☐	☐	☐
Poor eye contact	☐	☐	☐	☐
Does not catch on to social cues	☐	☐	☐	☐
Limited range of interests and interactions	☐	☐	☐	☐
Unusual sensitivity to sounds, touch, textures, movement, or taste	☐	☐	☐	☐
Coordination difficulties	☐	☐	☐	☐
Other (specify)	☐	☐	☐	☐

If the child is on medication, please answer the following questions:

Can you tell when the child is on medication or not?

Does the medication work consistently throughout the day?

Does the child appear to be on too much or too little medication?

Other comments:

Childhood Index of Executive Functions (ChIEF)

Child's Name:_ _

   Last,   First

Child's age: _ _ _ _ _ _ _ _ _ _ _ _   Gender: M/F

Relationship to child: _ _ _ _ _ _ _ _   Today's date:_ _ _/_ _ _/_ _ _ _

Considering your child's age, rate how well each statement applies to your child?

0 = Never/almost never   1 = Rarely/not often   2 = Frequently/often
3 = Always/most of the time

	0	1	2	3
(a) Needs persistent prompting to start homework.	☐	☐	☐	☐
(b) Homework somehow stops getting done when the adult leaves the scene.	☐	☐	☐	☐
(c) Is disorganized.	☐	☐	☐	☐
(d) Has a disastrous backpack unless someone else cleans it.	☐	☐	☐	☐
(e) Does not know all of the class assignments.	☐	☐	☐	☐
(f) Has a poor sense of how long a task will take.	☐	☐	☐	☐
(g) Is poor at anticipating his/her future needs. (Ex: Does not tell me about necessary school supplies well in advance of their being needed.)	☐	☐	☐	☐
(h) Can do homework and forget to hand it in.	☐	☐	☐	☐

		0	1	2	3
(i)	Does things that are not in his/her own self-interest, and "shoots him/herself in the foot." (Ex: angers people whose help he/she needs, or doesn't complete his/her own college applications.)	☐	☐	☐	☐
(j)	Has trouble learning from his/her mistakes. (Ex: getting an "F" for a missed assignment does not ensure that future homework is handed in on time.)	☐	☐	☐	☐
(k)	Has trouble noticing how others react to his/her behaviors.	☐	☐	☐	☐
(l)	Has trouble carrying out a sequence of commands (Ex: "Go brush your teeth, get dressed, and come down for breakfast.")	☐	☐	☐	☐
(m)	Has good intentions, but innately has problems executing a plan.	☐	☐	☐	☐
(n)	Overreacts easily and quickly.	☐	☐	☐	☐
(o)	Has anger that can be excessive (Ex: screams, throws things, gets red in the face, tightens fists.)	☐	☐	☐	☐
(p)	Is overly active physically (Ex: fidgety, out of seat, constantly touching everything.)	☐	☐	☐	☐
(q)	Must have his/her needs met immediately.	☐	☐	☐	☐
(r)	Is impulsive (acts before thinking).	☐	☐	☐	☐
(s)	Acts as if he/she has no brakes.	☐	☐	☐	☐
(t)	Has trouble shifting activities. (Ex: It is hard for my child to stop playing in order to come to dinner.)	☐	☐	☐	☐
(u)	Has trouble with self-control.	☐	☐	☐	☐
(v)	All of the above abilities are types of executive functions, which are the skills needed to control yourself in order to execute a plan. My child has trouble with executive functions.	☐	☐	☐	☐

Appendix 3

Further Reading
Books and Internet Resources

Attention deficit hyperactivity disorder (ADHD)
Books

Barkley, R.A. (1997) *ADHD and the Nature of Self Control.* New York: Guilford Press. More on the theory of ADHD, with some excellent practical advice. Fairly advanced reading.

Barkley, R.A. (2000) *Taking Charge of ADHD: The Complete, Authoritative Guide for Parents.* New York: Guilford Press. Dr. Barkley offers ground-breaking material on the nature of ADHD and executive functions. Harder, less optimistic reading.

Barkley, R.A. (2005) *Attention-Deficit Hyperactivity Disorder: A Handbook for Diagnosis and Treatment* (2nd edn). New York: Guildford Press. The scientific and unbelievably extensive literature review of ADHD, underlying Dr. Barkley's concepts. Like most medical "handbooks," it barely fits in your hand. Quite advanced reading.

Green, C. and Chee, K. (1997) *Understanding ADHD.* New York: Vermillion. This book addresses serious issues in an upbeat, even funny, style. A great place to start reading.

Hallowell, E.M. and Ratey, J.R. (1995) *Driven to Distraction.* New York: Simon and Schuster. This excellent book about ADHD has become the standard starting point, especially for adults with ADHD. Many parents might find themselves in this book.

Phelan, T.W. (1994) *Surviving Your Adolescents: How to Manage and Let Go of Your 13–18 Year Olds.* Glen Ellyn, IL: Child Management Press. Particularly useful for ADHD adolescents, who have a double dose of foresight blindness. Especially encouraging for ADHDer parents, because this book describes how many families of typical teenagers experience difficulty similar to their ADHD teen—and most of them seem to turn into normal adults.

Phelan, T.W. (2000) *All about Attention Deficit Disorder.* Glen Ellyn, IL: Child Management Press. All about ADHD for parents and teachers. Like all of his excellent books on childhood behavior, this book is both very useful and actually fun to read.

Silver, L.B. (1999) *Dr. Larry Silver's Advice to Parents of Children with ADHD.* California: Three Rivers Press. This text is particularly for ADHD and associated learning disabilities. Easy reading.

Zeigler Dendy, C. (2006) *Teenagers with ADD and ADHD: A Guide for Parents and Professionals.* Bethesda, MD: Woodbine House. Optimistic and practical advice for teenagers and others with ADHD. It features extensive sections on specific problems such as waking up and organization. There are also extensive lists of school (and home) accommodations.

Internet resources

www.ADDvance.com specializes particularly in girls and women with ADHD. They offer a wide range of excellent books. In particular, see their books *Understanding Girls with ADHD* and *Putting on the Brakes.*

ADDitude Magazine at www.additudemag.com is an electronic version of their excellent print magazine on ADHD.

ADDed Support at http://groups.msn.com/ADDedSupport/ is an active parent-to-parent message board.

AD(H)D Sanctuary at www.mhsanctuary.com has excellent links. In particular, see the Resource Page.

ADHD: 101 Tips for Teachers at www.dbpeds.org/articles/detail.cfm?id=31.

Behavioral Treatment of ADHD: An Overview by Dr. David Rabiner at www.athealth.com/Consumer/articles/Rabiner.html.

CHADD (Children and Adults with Attention Deficit Disorders) at www.chadd.org is an excellent, all-inclusive support group with local chapters. Phone: 800–233–4050.

Links on developing an IEP (Individual Educational Plan) at www.teach-nology.com/teachers/special_ed/iep/.

National Institutes of Health On-line booklet on ADHD at www.nimh.nih.gov/publicat/adhd.cfm.

www.chrisdendy.com site has useful teaching tips by Chris Zeigler Dendy.

www.ConductDisorders.com is another excellent parent-to-parent message board.

Newsletters via email (great ways to refresh your memory about caring for people with ADHD)

www.ADDchoices.com offers a newsletter for practical information on the spectrum of ADHD behaviors and problems.

www.ADDresource.com provides an ADHD newsletter and extensive source of further links.

www.ADHDnews.com has an empathically maintained and useful newsletter on
ADHD.

www.helpforADD.com by David Rabiner, Ph.D. is a very useful and
scientifically sound email newsletter.

Stormwatch Newsletter at www.adhdstormwatch.com has an upbeat monthly
newsletter on ADHD.

General neurobehavioral information
Books

American Psychiatric Association (2000) *Diagnostic and Statistical Manual of
Mental Disorders DSM-IV-TR* (4th edn, text revision). Washington, DC:
American Psychiatric Association. The "official" US diagnostic criteria for
mental disorders.

Kutscher, M.L., Attwood, T. and Wolff, R.R. (2005) *Kids in the Syndrome Mix of
ADHD, LD, Asperger's, Tourette's, Bipolar and More!: The One Stop Guide for
Parents, Teachers, and Other Professionals.* London: Jessica Kingsley Publishers.
The author's book on the full syndrome mix of conditions that often
accompany ADHD.

Pliszka, S.R., Carlson, C.L. and Swanson, J.M. *ADHD with Comorbid Disorders:
Clinical Assessment and Management.* New York: Guilford Press. Presents an
encyclopedic review of the literature on drug and behavioral treatments.
Intended for professional use.

Ratey, J.J. and Johnson, C. (1998) *Shadow Syndromes: The Mild Forms of Mental
Disorders that Sabotage Us.* New York: Bantam Books. This book explains that
many symptoms such as ADHD, obsessions, rage, autism, etc. can occur at
"subsyndromal" levels. Human brains are not "all or nothing."

Shore, K. (2002) *Special Kids Problem Solver: Ready-to-Use Interventions for Helping
All Students with Academic, Behavioral and Physical Problems.* San Francisco:
Jossey-Bass. The title says it all.

Wiener, J.M. and Dulcan, M.K. (eds) (2004) *Textbook of Child and Adolescent
Psychiatry* (3rd edn). Arlington, VA: American Psychiatric Publishing. This is
a professional level textbook.

Internet resources

www.ADDwarehouse.com carries a full selection of books for teachers and
parents on the whole spectrum of neurobehavioral disorders, not just
ADHD.

www.JKP.com is the website of Jessica Kingsley Publishers, which specializes in
children with special needs.

www.KidsBehavioralNeurology.com is Dr. Kutscher's website, featuring detailed information and links on most of the conditions covered in this book.

www.PediatricNeurology.com also hosts the information on conditions covered in this book, as well as other pediatric neurological issues such as headaches and seizures. Also authored by Dr. Kutscher.

Mental Health Links at www.baltimorepsych.com/consumer.htm has topics succinctly covered as part of a great psychiatry site produced by Northern County Psychiatric Associates.

www.NeuroPsychologyCentral.com has excellent links on neuropsychology topics.

Pediatric Psychiatry Pamphlets at www.klis.com/chandler/home.htm by Dr. Jim Chandler provide good natured, accessible, concise, responsible information on a large variety of conditions including ADHD, ODD, OCD, tics, panic, and bipolar disorders.

Learning Disabilities
Books

Osman, B.B. (1997) *Learning Disabilities and ADHD: A Family Guide to Living and Learning Together.* New York: Wiley.

Shaywitz, S. (2005) *Overcoming Dyslexia: A New and Complete Science-Based Program for Overcoming Reading Problems at Any Level.* New York: Vintage.

Internet resources

International Dyslexia Association at www.interdys.org. Mailing address: Chester Bldg, Suite 382, 8600 LaSalle Road, Baltimore, MD 21286. Phone: (800)-ABCD123.

LD on Line at www.ldonline.org is a superb resource including fair, full text, useful articles. Spend an evening there! Includes ADD, writing, learning, speech, and social difficulties. In particular, see their corner for kids.

National Center for Learning Disabilities at www.ld.org. Mailing address: 381 Park Ave. South Suite 1401, New York, NY 10016. Phone: (212)-545–7510.

www.Schwablearning.org has valuable brief articles covering a wide range of LD and associated problems.

Asperger's syndrome
Books

Attwood, T. (2007) *Asperger's Syndrome: A Guide for Parents*. London: Jessica Kingsley Publishers. The complete and updated diagnostic and treatment resource for Asperger's.

Bashe, P. and Kirby, B. (2001) *The OASIS Guide to Asperger Syndrome*. New York: Crown. Another excellent and complete resource (lengthy), written empathetically and fairly.

Willey, L.H. (1999) *Pretending to be Normal: Living with Asperger's Syndrome*. London: Jessica Kingsley Publishers. A powerful, elegant autobiography that traces the struggles faced by children and adults with Asperger's. Several appendices provide practical advice for students, employees, and parents.

Internet resources

The comprehensive OASIS website and support group at www.udel.edu/bkirby/asperger/ provides extensive information and peer support.

Dr. Tony Attwood's website at www.tonyattwood.com.au includes numerous excellent articles and an Asperger's rating scale.

Tourette's syndrome
Books

Dornbush, M. and Pruitt, S. *Teaching the Tiger*. Hope Press. This text is an entire book of accommodations for Tourette's students. Many of these ideas apply to ADHD and LD students as well.

Internet resources

Tourette Syndrome Association lists its local chapters at www.tsa-usa.org.

Tourette Syndrome—Plus at www.tourettesyndrome.net is a truly awesome, evidence-based, and practical site on Tourette's, OCD, rage, etc. by Leslie E. Packer, Ph.D.

Oppositional Defiant Behavior
Books

Barkley, R. (1998) *Your Defiant Child*. New York: Guilford Press. This is a book for caregivers of Oppositional/Defiant children by a careful researcher and thinker.

Greene, R.W. (2005) *The Explosive Child*. New York: HarperCollins. This a must read for parents of inflexible-explosive children who do not respond well to typical reward systems—whether or not they have Oppositional Defiant Disorder. This book is wonderfully and empathetically written.

Bipolar Depression
Books

Papolos, D. and Papolos, J. (2006) *The Bipolar Child* (3rd edn). New York: Broadway Books. This is an excellent diagnostic and treatment resource. This book has brought awareness about childhood bipolar disorder into the public realm.

Internet resources

www.bpkids.org is a great site on bipolar depression.

Sensory Integration Disorder
Books

Kranowitz, C.S. (1998) *The Out-of-Sync Child: Recognizing and Coping with Sensory Integration Dysfunction*. New York: Skylight Press. This book covers the diagnosis and treatment of sensory integration disorders. Makes sense out of a very broad topic.

Internet resources

Sensory Integration Dysfunction has understandable and complete information at www.tsbvi.edu/Outreach/seehear/fall97/sensory.htm.

References

American Psychiatric Association (2000) *Diagnostic and Statistical Manual of Mental Disorders DSM-IV-TR* (4th edn, text revision). Washington, DC: American Psychiatric Association.

Attwood, T. (2007) *The Complete Guide to Asperger's Syndrome.* London: Jessica Kingsley Publishers.

Barkley, R.A. (2000) *Taking Charge of ADHD: The Complete, Authoritative Guide for Parents.* New York: Guilford Press.

Barkley, R. A. (2005) *Attention-Deficit Hyperactivity Disorder: A Handbook for Diagnosis and Treatment* (2nd edn). New York: Guildford Press.

Barkley, R.A., Fischer M., Edelbrock, C. and Smallish, L. (1990) "The adolescent outcome of hyperactive children diagnosed by research criteria: An 8-year prospective follow-up study." *Journal of the American Academy of Child and Adolescent Psychiatry* 29, 546–557.

Bashe, P. and Kirby, B. (2001) *The OASIS Guide to Asperger Syndrome.* New York: Crown.

Bernstein, G. and Layne, A. (2004) "Separation anxiety and generalized anxiety disorder." In J. Wiener and M. Dulcan (eds) *Textbook of Child and Adolescent Psychiatry* (3rd edn). Arlington, VA: American Psychiatric Publishing, pp 557–575.

Brown T.E. (2005) *Attention Deficit Disorder: The Unfocused Mind in Children and Adults.* New Haven: Yale University Press.

Carver, J.M. (2005) "The Highway Patrol Approach to Discipline and Correction." Accessed 11/30/07 at www.drjoecarver.com/3/miscellaneous2.htm

Covey, S.R. (2000) *The 7 Habits of Highly Effective People.* New York: Running Press.

Geller, D.A., Biederman, J., Griffin, S., Jones, J. and Lefkowitz, T.R. (1996) "Comorbidity of juvenile obsessive-compulsive disorder with disruptive behavior disorders." *Journal of the American Academy of Child and Adolescent Psychiattry 35*, 12, 1637–1646.

Goldman, L.S.M., Genel, M., Bezman, R. and Spanetz, P. (1998) "Diagnosis and treatment of attention-deficit/hyperactivity disorder in children and adolescents." *Journal of the American Medical Association 279*, 1100–1107.

Greene, R.W. (2005) *The Explosive Child*. New York: HarperCollins.

Kranowitz, C.S. (1998) *The Out-of-Sync Child: Recognizing and Coping with Sensory Integration Dysfunction*. New York: Skylight Press.

Kutscher, M.L. (2002) *ADHD: Living Right Now!* White Plains, NY: Neurology Press.

Kutscher, M.L. (2006) *Children with Seizures: The Guide for Parents, Teachers, and other Professionals*. London: Jessica Kingsley Publishers.

Kutscher, M.L., Attwood, T. and Wolff, R.R. (2005) *Kids in the Syndrome Mix of ADHD, LD, Asperger's, Tourette's, Bipolar and More!: The One Stop Guide for Parents, Teachers, and Other Professionals*. London: Jessica Kingsley Publishers.

MTA Cooperative Group (1999) "A fourteen-month randomized clinical trial of treatment strategies for attention-deficit/hyperactivity disorder." *Archives of General Psychiatry 56*, 1073–1086.

Packer, A.J. (1997) *The Teenager's Guide to Good Manners, Proper Behavior, and Not Grossing People Out*. Minneapolis, MN: Free Spirit Publishing.

Papolos, D. and Papolos, J. (2006) *The Bipolar Child*, (3rd edn). New York: Broadway Books.

Phelan, T.W. (1994) *Surviving Your Adolescents: How to Manage and Let Go of Your 13–18 Year Olds*. Glen Ellyn, IL: Child Management Press.

Pliszka, S.R., Carlson, C.L. and Swanson, J.M. (1999) *ADHD with Comorbid Disorders: Clinical Assessment and Management*. New York: Guilford Press.

Rabiner, D. (2006) "Behavioral treatment for ADHD/ADD: A general overview." Accessed on 09/21/07 at www.helpforadd.com/behtreat.htm.

Quinn, P. (1995) *Adolescents and ADD: Gaining the Advantage*. Washington, DC: Magination Press.

Quinn, P. (2001) *ADD and the College Student: A Guide for High School and College Students with Attention Deficit Disorder* (revised). Washington, DC: Magination Press.

Quinn, P. and Stern, J. (2001) *Putting on the Brakes: Young People's Guide to Understanding Attention Deficit Hyperactivity Disorder* (revised). Washington, DC: Magination Press.

Ratey, J.J. and Johnson, C. (1998) *Shadow Syndromes: The Mild Forms of Mental Disorders that Sabotage Us*. New York: Bantam Books.

Silver, L.B. (1999) *Dr. Larry Silver's Advice to Parents of Children with ADHD*. California: Three Rivers Press.

Smith, B.H., Barkley, R.A. and Shapiro, C.J. (2006) "Attention-deficit/hyperactivity disorder." In E. Mash and R. Barkley (eds) *Treatment of Childhood Disorders* (3rd edn). New York: Guilford Press.

Waslick, B. and Greenhill, L. (2004) "Attention deficit/hyperactivity disorder." In J. Wiener and M. Dulcan (eds) *Textbook of Child and Adolescent Psychiatry* (3rd edn). Arlington, VA: American Psychiatric Publishing.

Wilens, T. E., Faracne, S.V., Biederman, J. *et al.* (2003) "Does stimulant therapy of attention deficit/hyperactivity disorder beget substance abuse? A meta-analytic review of the literature." *Pediatrics* 111, 179–185.

Willey, L.H. (1999) *Pretending to Be Normal: Living with Asperger's Syndrome.* London: Jessica Kingsley Publishers.

Zeigler Dendy, C. (2006) *Teenagers with ADD and ADHD: A Guide for Parents and Professionals.* Bethesda, MD: Woodbine House.

About the Author

Martin L. Kutscher MD is board certified in pediatrics and in neurology with special qualification in child neurology. Dr. Kutscher received his BA from Columbia University and his MD from Columbia University's College of Physicians and Surgeons. He completed a pediatric internship and residency at Temple University's St. Christopher's Hospital for Children. His neurology residency and pediatric neurology fellowship were completed at the Albert Einstein College of Medicine. He is currently a member of the Departments of Pediatrics and Neurology of New York Medical College. Dr. Kutscher has also been in private practice for more than 20 years. His practice is now limited to children with neurobehavioral problems, with offices in Rye Brook, Middletown, Wappingers Falls, and West Nyack, New York.

Dr. Kutscher has recently written three books: *ADHD BOOK: Living Right Now!* (Neurology Press, 2003), *Kids in the Syndrome Mix of ADHD, LD, Asperger's, Tourette's, Bipolar and More!: The One Stop Guide for Parents, Teachers, and other Professionals* (Jessica Kingsley Publishers, 2005), and *Children with Seizures: A Guide for Parents, Teachers, and other Professionals* (Jessica Kingsley Publishers, 2006). His website is www.KidsBehavioral Neurology.com, and he is also author of www.PediatricNeurology.com. Dr. Kutscher lectures internationally to doctor, teacher, therapist, and parent groups.

About the Illustrator

Douglas Puder MD is the illustrator for *The New York State Pediatrician* and is the editor/illustrator for the *Clarkstown Pediatrics Parentletter*. He is a practicing pediatrician with Clarkstown Pediatrics in Rockland County, New York.

Index